GW00870214

A Short His _y of Italy

A Short History of Italy

By

Mary Platt Parmele

Enhanced Media
2016

A Short History of Italy by Mary Platt Parmele. First published in *A Short History of Rome and Italy* by Mary Platt Parmele in 1901. This edition published 2016 by Enhanced Media.

Enhanced Media Publishing
Los Angeles, CA.

First Printing: 2016.

ISBN-13: 978-1530853304

ISBN-10: 1530853303

Contents

Chapter I

The time had passed when "Rome was the whole world, and all the world was Rome." That crater through which had poured the volcanic energies of the mighty empire was awfully still. But those energies were sleeping, not dead. The instinct for power, the old thirst for mastery, the same genius for organization, were finding a new pathway, and were preparing to convert the forlorn, dismantled city into the throne of a universal empire.

The least spiritual of nations was creating a spiritual kingdom, into which it would inject its own dominating strength. By controlling the sources of action, it might be master of men and of events. By holding the consciences and hearts of humanity in one hand, and the keys to heaven and hell in the other, a power might be wielded deep as human consciousness, and wide as the earth itself. There existed no such plan in the minds of the devout early bishops of Rome. But such was the instinctive process at work, as surely and as irresistibly as a mighty river if obstructed will find a new way to the sea. When before trembling souls were held up the horrors of eternal punishment, which might be remitted, and the tortures of purgatory shortened by gifts to the Church, money poured in great streams into the treasury. Dying sinners, even if half pagan, would leave their all, for the chance of purchasing forgiveness. This meant wealth and power never before possessed by a single organization. Ecclesiasticism was the road to success, and to be Bishop of Rome the richest prize offered to ambition, men still pagans at heart entering the lists to obtain it. The bishop, the custodian of this wealth, which he lavishly dispensed in charity and in deeds of mercy, was to the common people the adored father, or, as he began to be called, Papa (from the Greek), the word assuming in English the form "Pope."

The Greek and Oriental spirit which had come to pervade the Eastern Empire was making of Eastern Christianity something quite different from that of the West. There were different ideas of church government, and finally a different understanding of the dogmas of the Church concerning the nature of the Trinity. The assumption of headship by the Bishop of Rome, by virtue of an apostolic succession, was indignantly repudiated, and when the Pope asserted his authority by virtue of this headship to decide what were the dogmas of the faith, the Eastern Christians resolved upon a separation; and the Church of Christ on earth fell apart into two bodies—the Greek

Church, with its seat at Constantinople, and the Roman, to be enthroned at Rome.

It was a period of transition and of preparation. The rough foundations of future Europe were being laid. A Visigoth kingdom, established by Ataulf, held in subjection Romanized Spain. The Angles and Saxons had divided the Roman province of Britain between themselves and created a heptarchy which was to become a monarchy; Clovis, newly Christianized, had fastened a Frankish kingdom upon the Romanized and still pagan Gauls, and crowded the Visigoths over the Pyrenees. In Central Europe was a surging mass of Germanic tribes, never at rest, but with a general movement always toward the South, where their kinsmen, the Goths and Vandals, had already found homes of bewildering luxury ready for their use, and were fast acquiring the arts of civilization. In the region beyond, in the East, was another tumultuous mass of tribes, of which nothing was known yet— Slavonic, Finnish, Bulgarian, and strange Asiatic barbarians— all beginning to be drawn like moths toward the blazing illumination at Constantinople, the centre of that Byzantine Empire about which would revolve the ambitions and aspirations of what was to become Russia.

Although sundered in its spiritual life from the Empire of the West, Constantinople still claimed a shadowy political unity, and asserted an unsubstantial authority over the destinies of Rome and of Italy, which was for two centuries represented by an exarch at Ravenna, this exarchate being the nominal centre of Byzantine authority in the West.

But the Goths, barbarians though they were, did not learn of Christianity from Rome. More than a century before the fall of the empire they had received it in its primitive simplicity from Ulfilas, the Christian boy from Syria whom they had captured, and who created a Gothic alphabet and then translated his Bible into their tongue, explaining its truths in his own artless fashion, as they had been taught in his native land by Arius. The Roman Church had accepted, at the Council of Nice (327), the truth as expounded by Athanasius, making the Trinity the most sacred of its dogmas. So the Christianity of the Goths, which rejected the idea of the Trinity, was by Roman standards a very abominable heresy, and rivers of blood were to flow in Italy and in Spain before it was washed out by a triumphant trinitarianism.

The Gothic nation, like the Roman Empire, had separated into a Western and an Eastern division. And while the Visigoths had long since overrun Italy, Gaul, and Spain, the home of the Ostrogoths was still far north of the Danube. On the day of a great victory over the Huns, a son had been born to the King of the Ostrogoths. So the child of this good omen was called Theodoric—gift of God. When Odoacer became King of Italy, Theodoric was twenty-one years old. Seven hundred miles stretched between him and the throne of Italy, but he determined to possess it. By the year 492 he had wrenched the prize from Odoacer. He had not mistaken his strength nor his ability. Theodoric's is one of the few names to which by common consent has been attached the word "Great." When we compare this wise, enlightened, and humane reign with that of some of the human tigers who had worn the name of Caesar, we conclude that the barbarians brought something more than rugged strength into the expiring civilization. They brought some human elements which had been fatally lacking in the Romans. Terrible in wrath and in vengeance, the Goths had capacity for gentle emotions. Cruelty was their weapon, not their pastime. They did not with epicurean pleasure taste human blood with their wine. If Theodoric ordered the execution of his friend Boethius, the learned scholar, musician, and mathematician, it was because he believed he was trying to undermine the Arian faith, the religion of his people; but the remorse which overtook the barbarian king was the cause of his death (526 a.d.). The wife of this remarkable man was a sister of Clovis, and the magnificent monument erected by his daughter over his sarcophagus still remains at Ravenna.

With the strong hand of the king removed, Justinian, Emperor of the East, saw his opportunity to reconquer Italy. He sent his army, under Belisarina, and first captured Sicily. A few soldiers crawling through an abandoned aqueduct entered the city of Naples, and then opened the gates to the besieging army. Rome quickly surrendered, and the keys of the city were sent as a trophy to Constantinople (637). The Goths then in turn besieged Rome, and then it was that Hadrian's tomb, now the castle of St. Angelo, was first used as a fortress, and priceless statues (four thousand it is said), the work of famous Greek sculptors, were hurled from the walls, and fell crashing down upon the heads of the besieging Goths, so terrifying them that they fled.

When Justinian died, in 565, Italy was practically recovered. But the rule was oppressive, and some even desired a return of the Goths.

The Lombards were a fierce Germanic tribe originally from Northern Prussia, which had been, like all the others, gravitating toward Italy, watching an opportunity to slip inside that tempting garden through some open door. In the present conditions they saw their opportunity. Their descent into Northern Italy is still kept in remembrance by the name Lombardy, that beautiful region lying between the Alps and the Apennines. It was another instance of rugged untamed power coming out of the North to subdue the South. The terrified people fled before them, and by the end of the century these last barbarians had divided the peninsula with the Greek Empire. During the following century (the seventh) there were three centres of power in Italy— the Eastern Empire, which held Southern Italy and the eastern coast;

the Lombards, who were supreme in Northern Italy to the borders of Venetia; and the Pope. Among these three, it was the power of the Pope which was ascending. It knew no geographical, no political limits. It was as powerful in the Frankish kingdom and in Christianized Britain as at Rome. From the king on the throne to the humblest of the people, wherever there were true children of the Church, wherever there were stricken consciences or aching hearts, there were his subjects. The presence of Arianism was the greatest difficulty in the path, and the Church had been greatly strengthened by the conversion of Theodolinda, the wife of the King of the Lombards, to the true faith, and the consequent rejection of the Arian heresy by the Lombards. The famous "Iron Crown of Lombardy," now preserved near Milan, was a gift to the Lombard Queen from Gregory the Great in recognition of this service.

Precisely at this time there came into the world one of the greatest factors in shaping human events. Since Rome had raised the cross as a symbol of empire, the world had discovered the enormous power which might be wielded by holding the spiritual consciousness of man. The sincere purpose of Mahomet to replace a corrupt polytheism with a simple belief in one God, of whom he was the prophet, was seized upon by the wise and crafty Saracens. With the Koran in one hand, the sword in the other, and the crescent as their emblem, they determined to proselyte the world. They conquered Persia, Syria, and Egypt, and then swept along the African coast, effacing the Vandal Empire, not pausing until they reached the ocean. Their purpose of universal dominion was as much greater than Alexander's as the world was greater than the one in his time. The Church of Christ, which was the object of Saracen hatred, had two heads, and their plan included the destruction of both. They would enter Europe by the way of Spain, then cross the Pyrenees into France. Another Saracen host, after conquering Constantinople, would flow westward; and when the two streams met at Rome, the world would be theirs.

In 709 the movement began. The Visigoth Kingdom in Spain, now three centuries old, was swept out of existence, and a Moorish occupation of the Spanish peninsula began, which was to last seven hundred years. But at the Pyrenees the Saracens, or Moors as they are now called, were met by a Frankish army led by Charles Martel, which drove them back with such fury that there was never another attempt made to cross that barrier. Six hundred years were to elapse before the crescent would wave over Constantinople. But in all those years the shadow of the coming disaster would rest upon the Eastern Empire, which would be gradually weakened and exhausted by conflicts with her future destroyer.

Chapter II

Near the end of the eighth century the King of the Lombards captured Ravenna, and in annexing the territory which was the nominal seat of the imperial government, put an end to the exarchate which had existed for two centuries. Alboin's ambition was now fired to achieve a greater triumph, i.e., a complete ascendancy in the peninsula. This attempt, in itself so fruitless, changed the whole course of European history. The Merovingian kings were faithful sons of the Church, so the Pope appealed to the Pranks to protect him from the Lombard encroachments, and Pepin, the son of Charles Martel, came twice across the Alps with an army, checked the ambition of the Lombards by a conquest which made him virtual sovereign, then, upon leaving, cast an imperial gift into the lap of the Church—five cities and a vast extent of territory. This, known as the Donation of Pepin, was the beginning of the temporal kingdom of the popes in Italy. Pepin, Maire du Palais of the last Merovingian king, resolved, since he held the kingly power, also to assume the kingly crown. Pope Zacharias, in gratitude for his gift to the Church, sanctioned the audacious act, and sent his representative to place the symbol of power upon the head of his faithful son.

When Pope Adrian I again needed protection from the Lombards, a greater than Pepin wore the crown he had snatched from the Merovingian. His son Charlemagne was King of the Franks. The tie uniting the Eastern Empire and the Western was worn to a frail thread; with hostile religions, and characters which had grown utterly divergent, the union was a mockery. The wretched Irene, who put out the eyes of her own son in order that she might reign, was disgracing the throne. Charlemagne's services to the Church were unequalled. A man who could compel a whole army of pagan Saxons to be baptized in an afternoon, and Christianize a nation in a campaign, was the sort of ally the Pope needed. So when Pope Adrian I. asked for protection, Charlemagne, with fully matured plans, came himself, and with the consent and acquiescence of the Pope, he took formal possession of Italy, and the centre of power returned from the East to the West.

On Christmas Day in the year 800, Charlemagne knelt before the high altar at St. Peter's in Rome, while Leo III. placed upon his head the crown which made him "By the Grace of God, Emperor of the Romans and of the Holy Roman Empire." By these words the present was deftly linked to the past, and Charlemagne bad become the successor of Augustus and of Constantine. The line of Caesar which had been prolonged in the East would be continued through Charlemagne's successors in the West. The Roman Church, instead of being politically joined to its enemy, was in natural alliance with its most ardent and powerful defender. In the compact formed between the Emperor and the Pope there was a mutual dependence. The election of the Pope required the sanction of the Emperor. Nor was the King of the Pranks emperor until crowned by the Pope. In this friendly clause there lurked material for many troubled centuries, and the writing of many histories. The wonder is that a statesman as astute as Charlemagne did not, as a condition, then and there fix the question of supremacy. But he did not realize the extraordinary nature of the power with which he was in alliance, any more than did the Pope suspect the turn of events which would make him the vassal of German emperors. Upon the death of Charlemagne, his empire was divided among his sons into three parts. Louis took the Eastern and German Franks, Charles the Western and Latinized Franks, and to Lothar was assigned the imperial title together with Italy, and a long narrow strip of territory extending to the North Sea. Instead of being in natural and close alliance with Latinized France, Italy found herself irrevocably tied to the Germans, a Teutonic people with which she had nothing in common.

The great states of modern Europe had now all come into being. Italy, France, Spain, from their infancy nourished by currents from the ancient world, were the children and the heirs of Latin civilization. England, Germany, Russia, all born in this pregnant century, were in no way linked with the past. They were children of new and obscure parentage. Of the Roman occupation in Britain there remained not a trace after the coming of the Angles and Saxons. Germany, the one state where Roman power could not get a foothold, had not an ancestral root extending beyond her native soil; while Russia, the strangest ethnic product of all, the Slav blended with utterly unknown Asiatic fragments, was going to sit at the feet of the expiring Byzantine Empire and learn its first lesson in civilization. It was at the very time Charlemagne was being crowned at Rome, in the year 800, that the heptarchy in Britain was consolidated and King Alfred reigned over England. The treaty of Verdun in 840 created Germany; and in 862 a few Slavonic tribes were brought into political union by the Scandinavian Rurik, who reigned as Grand Prince at Kieff, over what was to become Muscovite Russia.

By the eleventh century feudalism had organized new social conditions in all of these states (except Russia). Great nobles in Germany dwelt in castles which were also their strongholds in the private wars which prevailed. The narrow strip of territory extending to the North Sea had widened and grown into a powerful and compact kingdom; while Italy was the prey of anarchy and disorders, led by aristocratic factions in league with a Church growing every year more corrupt. Needing the political tie binding her to Germany, she none the less hated it. On the other hand, the authority of the popes, although sometimes appealed to in disputes concerning the succession, was detested by the Germans, and the necessity of going to Rome for the imperial crown was so exasperating that some preferred to dispense with it. A deep antagonism was developing between emperors and popes. The Church had become unspeakably corrupt. For a long period the character of nearly every occupant of the papal chair had been stained with vice too gross to be described, and the name Holy Father had become a mockery.

The very enormity of the condition produced a reaction. A party of reform came into existence in Italy, led by the fiery monk Hildebrand. An ascetic, with exalted ideas of the sanctity and the authority of the papal office, he made two things his determined aim: the purification of the Church, and divesting the Emperor of the power of investiture or the bestowal of the papal dignity —a privilege not often exercised, but prized for its potential usefulness.

When Hildebrand became Pope Gregory VII., a still larger purpose developed. He it was who first made the monstrous claim that not alone German emperors, but all sovereigns, were subject to the Pope, and bound by his decisions. Christ was the King of Kings; and the Pope's authority was absolute in Christendom, and from it there was no appeal.

Henry IV., Emperor of Germany, in some dispute had asked Pope Gregory's interposition. In reply, the Pope imperiously commanded the Emperor's immediate presence at Rome to answer charges against himself. The long-impending crisis had come. The point Charlemagne had failed to determine, whether Pope or Emperor was the greater, Hildebrand was going to decide for all time.

Henry not only indignantly refused to obey, but deposed the Pope. Whereupon the Pope excommunicated Henry.

One can scarcely realize now what this meant at that time. Excommunication was a word before which the strongest quailed. It was not only eternal torture hereafter, but a living death here. The excommunicated was cut off from human association; people approached him at their peril; the clothes he wore, the dishes from which he ate, were polluted. He was a moral leper. Henry's subjects threatened to elect a new emperor unless he made his peace at once with the offended Church. So, as has been often told, the royal penitent started in midwinter upon his famous pilgrimage to Canossa, in coarsest garb, bare-headed, barefooted, standing for three days outside the castle walls waiting for forgiveness and absolution (1073 A.D.).

Such was the power of the Church when in 1095 the kingdoms of Europe enrolled themselves under its banners to recover the Holy Sepulchre from the Saracens. The principle of unity of which ancient Rome was the monstrous embodiment had passed into the spiritual empire which was its successor. How could there be political growth in Italy with a man arrogating to himself divine powers enthroned in the very heart of the peninsula, before whose authority kings and armies trembled? What political organization could stand with a papal kingdom as its centre? There might be kingdoms and principalities and small centres of power outside of it—if not too ambitious and outreaching. And that is just what there were going to be for many, centuries.

At this period the restless people who had for a century occupied the province of Normandy in France under promise of good behavior, were looking about for new fields of adventure. While William, Duke of Normandy, was eagerly watching the turn of affairs just across the channel in England, his knights were roaming the Mediterranean shores, offering their services sometimes to the Greek Empire in fighting the Saracens, sometimes to Southern Italy in repelling the Greek Empire. A certain Tancred d'Hauteville had ten of these adventurous sons, who had in this way become practically masters of Magna Graecia, all the fruits of their knightly adventures finally coming into the hands of one son, Robert, known as Robert Guiscard (or the crafty), who, as head of a great dukedom embracing all of Southern Italy, now became a power to be reckoned with. When his younger brother, Roger, wrested Sicily from the Saracens, the fair island was reunited with Italy, forming one kingdom with Naples, over which a later Roger Guiscard was crowned by the Pope, King of Naples, or, as it was thereafter known, the kingdom of the two Sicilies. While the host of Norman knights were following William into England, a smaller host were streaming southward, bringing the same brilliant receptiveness and masterful energy into Italy, where they were going to survive as in France, and in England, and in Russia, not as a race, but as an element.

So in the twelfth century, with the Norman Kingdom in the south, and the Lombard Kingdom in the north of Italy, the Papal Territory and the independent state of Venice represented all of authority that was Italian.

Since the crusades the European states had been drawn into a closer relation; the currents of political sentiment in one country would flow into another, and thus great tides or waves of tendency would roll over the Continent as if it were one organism. One of these movements was the rise of free cities in Spain, France, Germany, and Italy. It had its origin in a desire for some refuge from the everlasting unrest, from the eternal conflict, where small communities, still acknowledging the paramount authority, might behind their own walls work out their own problem of government and development. A remarkable group of free cities had formed in Lombardy. The *burghers* shut themselves behind their walls from the general political storm, and also from the exaction and oppressions of feudal lords, whose fortresses studded the country; then they would cautiously open the gates to someone among the superior class whom they believed would strengthen them, and bestow upon him a seat or an office in their government council. Such was the process by which they had grown. Milan, which was the oldest, largest, and most important of the group, assumed a headship. No idea of combination existed. The disintegrating fires of envy, jealousy, and hatred were at work keeping the cities as far apart from each other as had been Athens and Sparta. Milan tried to annihilate Lodi, and the little Cremona had a still smaller victim in the little city of Croma. It was the old story of the Greek republics. Times had been bad enough without this needless civil war, with twelve armed invasions by the emperors of Germany in two centuries, putting down as many attempts to set up their own Italian kings in Lombardy! A crisis finally came when Lodi in desperation appealed to the Emperor Frederick I.—the great Barbarossa. When the Emperor sustained Lodi in her quarrel with Milan, that imperious city refused to submit to his dictation. The Emperor had been watching these small centres of political freedom, which had cast off their feudal allegiance, and the allegiance to their bishop. Now they were defying him. He meant to teach a lesson which would not be forgotten. He marched down to the rebellious city and literally tore it to pieces; then invited the neighboring cities to come and help themselves to the fragments; which they did with such ferocious zeal that nothing remained. Milan, the beautiful city, the pride of Lombardy, was effaced. Such extravagant vengeance produced a sympathetic reaction. The Milanese were assisted to rebuild their city, and to guard against future tyrannical interference from Emperor Frederick, there was formed a league of twenty-five cities. This is the famous Lombard League to which the great Barbarossa yielded in 1113, when he conceded the rights of individual cities to govern themselves, the general sovereignty of the Emperor at the same time remaining unimpaired.

Chapter III

The life of the Norman Kingdom in Italy was brief as it was brilliant. Constance, the daughter of King Roger I., married Henry, son of Barbarossa. So in the absence of a male heir, before the end of the twelfth century, the whole territory acquired by the Guiscard brothers was transferred to Henry VI., then Emperor of Germany, who now claimed to hold in his hand all of Italy excepting only the papal dominions, the independent state of Venice, and the free cities of the North. Pope Urban IV., after a prolonged and fruitless attempt to prevent such a calamity, invited Charles, Duke of Anjou, brother of Louis IX. of France (the saint), to come and wear the crown of Naples and Sicily. Charles accepted the invitation, drove out Manfred, the illegitimate son of Frederick II, and was proclaimed king of the Two Sicilies. The wretched chapter closes with two tragedies—one pathetic, the other colossal. The last of the Hohenstaufens, Conradin, a boy sixteen years old, came with an army and with banners and with enthusiasm to claim his own and drive out the usurper. He was defeated and delivered to Charles, who dared not take the chances of leaving alive so winning and so just a claimant to his throne. On the shore of the Bay of Naples the scaffold was erected. After a brief prayer the boy threw his glove among the weeping friends near him, as if it were a charge to avenge his death, then gave himself to the executioner.

So detested did the rule of the French become that it needed only a spark to start a conflagration. An insult offered by a French officer to a Sicilian maiden on her way to vespers with her affianced husband precipitated the outbreak which had been for some time preparing. The officer was killed on the spot, and a massacre of the French in Palermo instantly began, the contagion spreading to other towns, until not a Frenchman remained in the island. This, known as the Sicilian Vespers, occurred in 1282. The island of Sicily was taken away from Charles, and bestowed by the Pope upon Pedro III., King of Arragon, Naples remaining to Charles.

So now there were three foreign masters in Italy, and the free cities instead of drawing closer together for mutual protection were wasting their strength in embittered rivalries, each of these cities at the same time being rent asunder by strife between the two political parties, the Guelfs and Ghibellines. There had arisen in the twelfth century two political parties the party of the Pope, and the party of the Emperor. The adherents of the Pope were called Guelfs, and those of the Emperor, Ghibellines. These names gradually outgrew their original significance and came to express two opposing tendencies; tendencies which we should now call conservative and radical. The Guelfs stood for a new Italy, with feudalism effaced, commerce fostered, and a leaning toward republicanism. The name Ghibelline stood for a protest against any changes in the old order of things. But what these names chiefly represented was an unintelligent destructive force. They afforded banners under which people could enroll their selves in carrying on traditional feuds and private hatreds, joining this or that faction as it would help them to build up or to ruin. The long and purposeless struggle between Guelfs and Ghibellines was even more detrimental to Italy than foreign oppression, because it was disintegrating, a quality which opens the shortest road to dissolution.

While the history of the Italian peninsula in ancient times is a single thread, it had now become a strand composed of many threads of almost equal value. Venice, Florence, Pisa, Genoa, and Milan formed a group of autonomous states which seemed more like the children of Greece than of Rome. Each was an intense expression of political individualism. Each was grasping for power and wealth and territory, and with a strange instinct for beauty, lavish in expenditure for embellishment, they were vying with each other in the growing splendor of their cities. In Florence, Pisano and Cimabue were already teaching the principles of the art of beauty, and the stately group of buildings which men still travel far to see were rearing their heads. Venice, looking across the Adriatic toward Greece and the Orient, had for two centuries been studying art at the feet of the greatest masters. As "she sat in state throned on her hundred isles," the Church of St. Mark's and a multitude of shining palaces had already arisen from the waves, which gave back their shimmering reflections Just as they do today. These marvellous creations were clothed in the garment of an ancient civilization, the "spoils of nations," from "the exhaustless East," which the conquering Venetians had brought bodily to make their city beautiful, as should be the Bride of the Sea! This splendor of adornment tells the story of conquest and outreaching power and of commercial success which made it possible, and which made Venice the object of jealous hatred to Pisa, her sister city on the Mediterranean, who also had her own brilliant conquests and prosperity, owning the islands of Sardinia (taken from the Moors), Elba, and a large part of Corsica, besides colonies in the East, all of which riches, on the other hand, excited the envious hatred of Genoa, which was to be the cause of her final downfall.

The situation of Florence was less favorable for the extension of her borders than for development within herself. The fertility of her soil, the perfection of her climate, and perhaps the slight retirement from the restless sea, centred her energies in the productive industries which were the source of her enormous wealth and lasting vitality. As the merchants, the wealth-producing class, were not noble, there was a constant recruiting of the energies of the state from below, a process which always insures long life, so that a plebeian plutocracy, although a present evil, is apt to be a future good.

All these cities had in their administration a shadowy survival of ancient Rome, with their two consuls, and a senate elected by the people. But on account of the distracting quarrels of the Guelfs and Ghibellines it became necessary to devise a new system, and then came into existence a chief magistrate with dictatorial powers, called *podesta*. This official was always a stranger, who on account of known probity and wisdom was invited to come and govern them for one year. During this period he must not enter the house of any private citizen, nor must he bring with him his family. This solitary person was expected by these restrictions to be kept safe from pernicious local influences. While ingenious and perhaps to some extent wise, this was, however, teaching the people to be submissive to a possible tyrant.

Later, in order to defend themselves from the insolence of the nobility, the people created another singular functionary, called the gonfalonier, or bearer of the standard (*gonfalon*). His duty, like that of the tribunes, was to suppress attacks on the liberties of the people, an army of men always standing ready the instant he hung out his gonfalon, to rush to his aid against any refractory noble.

In no other city did party feeling run so high between Guelf and Ghibilline as in Florence, the victory of one faction meaning unsparing vengeance upon the other. Of course the conflict of classes and private feuds and personal aims became intermingled and entangled with the larger classification. A system devised to hold the turbulent elements in check was finally adopted, which lasted for two centuries. Twelve men, called the *Signoria*, were elected once in two months, who acted as aids to the podesta. The Florence of this period had its learned class, who, under the shadow of the rising Duomo, and the Baptistery, discussed the opposing views of Aquinas and Duns Scotus, or, as is even more likely, the marvellous tales brought from the fabled East by the Venetian traveller Marco Polo, or the latest utterance of their hot-headed and erratic townsman, Dante. As the sympathies of the present day naturally turn to the Guelfic party of that time, it is something of a shock to learn that Dante was intensely Ghibelline or imperialistic. He was elected in 1300 one of the priors of the republic; that is, a member of the Signoria or grand council. While he was at one time absent at Rome upon official business, the Guelfic party triumphed, and he, with the rest, was condemned to have his property confiscated, and for him was added the promise that he would be burnt alive if he ever returned to Florence. So, homeless, and in poverty, and in bitterness of heart, the exile completed the Divine Comedy which he had commenced, in rage deep but impotent using his pen, the only weapon with which he could strike back, by holding up to execration forever the men who had ruined him, and who, as he believed, were destroying his beloved Florence.

Pisa had also her duomo, baptistery, and her leaning tower proudly rearing their heads. The story of Count Ugolino shows what sort of hearts dwelt in this Ghibelline city. This nobleman to whom had been confided the state at a time of great peril, improved the opportunity to establish a tyranny of his own. His treachery was discovered, and the wrath of the people may be measured by the punishment inflicted, which Dante has pictured with such fearful power. Ugolino, his two sons and two grandsons were thrown into prison. After the look had been turned upon them, the key was thrown into the Arno, and the five were left to perish slowly by starvation. It needed not the imagination of a Dante to make an "Inferno" of such a lingering tragedy. The power of Pisa had been sapped by a long struggle with Genoa, and in 1241, after a naval defeat at the month of the Arno, so completely was she stripped of her former glory, that it was said, "If you would see Pisa, you must go to Genoa."

After the fourth crusade, one might truly have said, If you would see Constantinople, you must go to Venice. A great Christian host which had gathered with the purpose of making one more attempt to recover Palestine had assembled at Venice, where they awaited the money required for the expedition. Finally, as it did not come, Dandolo, the Doge of Venice, offered to supply the required amount if instead of Palestine they would make Zara, a rebellious Venetian town on the eastern coast of the Adriatic, their first objective point. This having been done, the infamous proposition was next artfully made, as they still needed money, that they join the Venetians in an attack upon Constantinople, where there was an empty throne standing between two contestants. The result of this was that an army of crusaders with the avowed purpose of pillage took possession of Constantinople, and after committing every outrage which can attend the sacking of a city, they bore away to Venice an amount of plunder which cannot be estimated, and which still clothes the city of the winged lion with gold and silver and jewels and priceless works of art. The four bronze horses, which adorn the portal to St. Mark's Church, were a part of this disgraceful spoil. They are said to have been made during the reign of either Nero or Trajan by Roman workmanship.

Venice, which was the oldest of the autonomous states, had hitherto eared little for extension in Italy, her ambitions and desires all turning toward the East, which possessed for her such a fascination. But in the thirteenth century a struggle commenced with Genoa, which lasted for thirty years. Her Duke, or Doge, was elected by the people, as was also the Senate, which shared his authorities. Gradually the democratic principle had been disappearing, and an aristocratic body called the Grand Council was by degrees absorbing the powers of government, the Senate finally becoming hereditary in a few families. It was when not yet fully in the clutches of her aristocracy, when her merchant princes were the carriers for the world, and when, sitting at the gateway leading to the East, she was taking toll for the traffic of Europe, that Venice reached the height of her glory.

Chapter IV

The century just closing had wrought many changes in Europe. It had given to England the foundation for her liberties in the Magna Charta. In France the period of free cities had passed, and the principle of monarchy was gaining upon a waning feudalism. The descendants of the Visigoth kings of Spain as they fought their long crusade of centuries, were slowly crowding the Moors down toward their last stronghold in the province of Granada, In Germany the house of Hohenstaufen had given place to the house of Hapsburg. Russia was in the grasp of the Mongols, but with a steady impulse toward power of a phenomenal sort, the nebulous mass was preparing to revolve about its new centre at Moscow.

To none had the thirteenth century been more significant than to the papal empire at Rome. When Pope Innocent III brought that odious tyrant, King John of England, cringing to his feet, Hildebrand's claim of papal supremacy bad been established. That contumacious King refused to accept an Archbishop of Canterbury appointed by the Pope. Then Innocent III absolved John's subjects from their allegiance to him, and handed his kingdom over to the King of France (1213 a.d.). When the terrified John came crouching before him, whether the Pope was or was not king of kings was no longer a question. But the papal power had reached its climax and the fourteenth century saw a rapid decline which there was no Gregory VII nor Innocent III to arrest. A long wrangle between Philip IV of France and Pope Boniface VII., over the papal prerogatives, was terminated by the accession of a French archbishop to the chair of St. Peter, under the name of Clement V. Faithful to the cause of his sovereign, Clement removed the papal residence from Rome to Avignon, a town within the French borders, where seven popes successively lived and ruled directly under French influences. This in the annals of the Church is known as the Babylonian Captivity, a curious hiatus which lasted just seventy years (1309-79), and which cast a dark cloud over the Church for a century.

Henry VII, who had just succeeded to the throne of Germany (1311 a.d.), thought this a favorable time to go to Rome for his imperial crown. He could at the same time strengthen the bonds of amity with his Italian kingdom, and also aid his Gaelfic friends in trying to drive out the Ghibellines, who now had possession in Florence. Before the attack upon Florence the Emperor suddenly and mysteriously died. The Guelfs asserted that poison had been put into a cup of sacramental wine offered him after his coronation by the papal legate. However this may be, his death was the signal for hostilities fiercer than had ever before existed, a frantic hatred driving Guelfs and Ghibellines to the most extravagant excesses. King Robert of Naples also saw in the absence of the Pope and the prevailing disorder an opportunity to subjugate all of Italy to Angevine rule by using Guelfs and Ghibellines to destroy each other, thus fighting the nation with its own fires. But he was not strong enough for so ambitious a design.

In the midst of this general anarchy, Rome had her own special type of disorder. Her government (so called) consisted of a chief magistrate, or senator, with powers similar to the podesta, and a council somewhat like the ancient Senate. Guelfs and Ghibellines at Rome were neither for the Pope nor against him. They were for the Colonnas, or the Orsinis. The politics of the city revolved about the eternal strife existing between these two noble families. Like all the great nobles in Rome, these families were descended from robber barons, some Scandinavian, some from the Rhine, some from Southern Italy. With no patrician blood, they were the apex of that pyramid which feudalism had planted upon Rome, and represented the system which it was the aim of the Guelfs to exterminate.

Petrarch, who was admitted to the closest intimacy with the Colonnas, has made the world well acquainted with them, so we know what refinements, grace, and charm there were in the ladies of that princely house, and also what noble princely virtues existed in the men. But as they fought with the Orsinis for the grand prize, the senatorship, there was not a throb of patriotism, not a single thought of Rome or Romans in the breasts of these splendid medieval princes. So when the popes were exiled to Avignon, the city was given up to lawlessness. Scenes of violence and terror were of common occurrence upon the streets. Not a woman or a child was safe in the city at night, nor was anyone safe at any time outside the walls, where the Campagna was infested with robbers, and the Tiber with pirates.

There was a youth growing up in Rome at this time, who was pondering upon these things. He was the son of an inn-keeper and of a washerwoman, but eager to know, and with keen intelligence he read, and read again the story of the ancient republic, its heroes, its triumphs, its noble ideals. This was Cola di Rienzi. Gradually there formed in his mind a dream, the dream of a rebirth of the splendid ancient Rome—which would be a new Rome with a soul, a Christian soul— which might again be mistress of the world! He must first arouse the people to a sense of their degradation—then he would lead them to the great consummation. He— Cola di Rienzi—would be the liberator, and lift Rome from her degradation to a throne—higher than ever before, because it would be a Christian throne. He had the gift of eloquence, and perhaps another mysterious gift which we now call personal magnetism. His enthusiasm, his intensity, the magic of his speech, gained listeners to his vague exalted dream about what he called the "good estate," when law and order should prevail, and all men have justice in a city which had taken her place again as mistress of the world. By painted allegories which he displayed upon the streets, and by juggling with the imaginations of the people, and by persistence and eloquent speech, he rose step by step, inspiring even the Pope with a belief in his ability to accomplish a miracle, and completely capturing the heart and the imagination of Petrarch. It seemed as if he were inspired, and as if his audacious plan developed by magic. Without a drop of blood, or a blow, the revolution was effected. The nobles, although angry and sullen, seemed awed by a mysterious force, and offered no resistance. A republic was proclaimed, with Rienzi at its head, under the modest title of Tribune.

The golden age seemed to have come. Every promise was fulfilled. The roads were cleared of highwaymen, and the river of pirates. Peace reigned in the city. Rienzi, robed in scarlet, sat in the Capitol, his palace, and listened to complaints from high and low, dealing impartial justice to all. The Pope at Avignon was pleased, and the people at Rome seemed mad with joy, and believed the millennium was at hand. The news spread over Europe and into Asia. The Great Potentate at Babylon, hearing that a man of wonderful justice had arisen in Rome, made supplication to Mahomet to protect Jerusalem from this new danger!

Dreamy visionary though he may have been, unbalanced though he certainly was, Rienzi had sent an electric thrill throughout the world. If only a kind fate could have taken him then! The intoxication of power began to work and to manifest itself in more severity, more splendor, more confiscations of the treasures of the nobles to adorn his own palace. The great barons were now obliged to stand uncovered in his presence while he sat, and the people began to tremble before him. He devised strange fantastic ceremonies investing himself with higher and higher dignities, and finally with a silver crown and sceptre, the nobles and the Pope's legate, still under his spell, assisting in the splendid pageant. The strange story of self-intoxication and extravagant pretension, in fantastic theatrical garb, begins to seem more like the libretto of a comic opera than sober history; and yet all was taken seriously by the Pope, and by sovereigns in Europe. But his friends were alarmed. Petrarch, who had almost severed his intimate friendship with the Colonnas for his sake, no longer wrote him daily letters telling him he was greater than Romulus, greater than Brutus, or Camillus. He solemnly warned him—entreated him to pause and to remember that he was "not lord, but simply minister, of the republic."

Rome was tranquil, but it was cowed, and beneath the adulation there was an undertone of anger. But Rienzi heard it not, and prepared for the climax. He announced to the Italian cities that henceforth they would be governed from Rome alone, and he conferred Roman citizenship upon every native of Italy. This was a splendid dream of empire and of a united Italy, which was to be realized five centuries later. But Rienzi's dream was more than that; it was of an unlimited and impossible empire of which he in some mystic way was to be the head, not of Italy but of Christendom. The early nobility of his purpose had vanished. Instead of the "wise and clement," as he was once called, he was changing into a blood-thirsty tyrant who gloated over the dead bodies of two Colonnas slain in an affray with his troops. His treatment of the nobles became atrocious. The Pope was alarmed and angry, and deposed him. At the signs of a popular uprising, the fallen Tribune fled to the Apennines. Seven years later he made his peace with the Pope, who once more commissioned him to restore distracted Rome to tranquillity. He put on the airs of an emperor, drank heavily, became gross and arrogant. As he sat in his palace one morning, flushed with wine, a strange sound reached his ears, the noise of a tumult below, then he heard the terrible words, "Death to the traitor, Rienzi!" He attempted flight disguised as a shepherd, stained his face, mingled with the shouting crowd of people below, joining his voice with theirs in execration of himself. But the light flashed upon his jewelled bracelets which he had forgotten to remove. He was recognized, dragged to the great stair, and at the foot of the Lion where death sentences were usually read, was stabbed to death.

Chapter V

That great region lying south of the Alps known as Lombardy was composed of an imposing group of principalities—Milan, Verona, Mantua, Padua, and the duchies of Ferrara and Modena. Milan, the most powerful of these, had for over a century been arbitrarily and mercilessly ruled by one family, the Viscontis. The city of Milan, and also Verona, with no ambitions beyond the peninsula, were, like that other inland city of Florence, the opulent centres of trade and manufacture, their aims and policy entirely different from the two great cities lying south of them.

Genoa and Venice had grown by foreign conquest; were both majestic maritime powers, both seeking the same markets by the same great highways. Both had factories skirting the entire coast of the Black Sea, and both were bringing spices from Arabia, and precious merchandise from India, and grain and furs from Russia. Separated from each other by the whole width of Italy, it was in the eastern waters that these rival cities fought their long battle of a half century, sometimes Venice on her knees to Genoa, and sometimes Genoa supplicating Venice for mercy. It was in the earlier days of this struggle that Marco Polo, upon returning from his twenty-five-year trip in Cathay, threw his fortune and himself into the contest with the Genoese, and after a calamitous defeat was carried with ship-loads of other prisoners to Genoa. One year spent in the Genoese dungeon gave to the world an epoch-making book. His marvellous stories would soon have faded from the memory of man, had not a fellow-prisoner pieced together the wonder-tale as it was simply and unaffectedly told by the traveller, and thus produced the book which so profoundly affected the imaginations of men for centuries, and which lured Columbus into his audacious attempt to reach the great Kublai Khan by sailing into the West!

Venice, as Queen of the Adriatic, claimed the right of exclusive navigation in that sea, her sovereignty being every year renewed and proclaimed by an imposing symbolic ceremony in which the Doge, representing Venice, wedded the Adriatic with a ring. Genoa resisted this claim of exclusive ownership of the sea, and it was a proud moment for her in 1352 when she destroyed the Venetian fleet and the humbled Doge sent ambassadors to the Genoese admiral with a blank sheet of paper, begging him to dictate his own terms for peace. But the too-confident victor replied contemptuously, "You shall have no peace till we have bridled those horses of yours on the place of St. Mark." The Venetians gathered themselves for a supreme effort. The

Genoese standard was already floating from the towers of Chioggia near Venice, with the Lion of St. Mark reversed in token of defeat. Precious works of art, those spoils of Constantinople, were melted for the gold and silver. The Venetian women gave their jewels, and the nobles their plate. After a long and brave struggle the Genoese fleet was at their mercy, and instead of "bridling the horses" at St. Mark's, Genoa fell to the position of a second-rate maritime power in Italy, from which she never again arose. In her consternation she appealed to Milan for protection, and a Milanese governor took the humiliated city in charge.

With Milan as an ally, the conflict with Venice was renewed, and the Venetian fleet destroyed. The great Visconti who was then lord of Milan, flushed with this triumph, began to extend his mailed hand over the rest of the principalities, and was by 1385 master of Lombardy. To escape this hard fate the Lombard states combined with Venice in an appeal to the German Emperor. So when the curtain again rises upon this troubled stage, we see one more source of devastation— Charles IV with his soldiers tramping over the depleted and exhausted Italian states, and while on his way to Rome to receive his imperial crown, wearing that oft-transferred and rather mysterious symbol of power, the "Iron Crown of Lombardy!"

Out of the fratricidal strife Venice had emerged stronger than before, Milan had arisen with greatly augmented prestige, while Genoa had fallen from her great elevation to the rank of a second-rate power. Venice during the prolonged struggle had passed completely into the hands of her aristocracy. The people had already been excluded from her Grand Council. But the meshes were to be drawn still closer. From this body was selected a "Council of Ten" (1311 a.d.), a mysterious organization, the functions of which have never been fully understood. But with their methods the world is entirely familiar. The secrecy of the trials, the absence of witnesses, the ignorance of the victims of the charges brought against them, has made the very name of this tribunal a synonym for mysterious horror and cruelty. Men and women occupying the highest positions would disappear to be heard of never more. And no one dared ask whither they had gone, or why! Impartial as fate, it struck the powerful as well as the weak. Indeed it seems to have been at first designed as a check upon ambitions and conspiring nobles, and then to have extended its scope indefinitely. But a succession of conspiracies for the overthrow of the government probably led to the creation of this monstrous court of justice, so-called.

The memory of one of the latest and most celebrated of these conspirators is still kept alive in the Ducal Palace at Venice, where among a series of portraits representing seventy-six Doges, one empty panel painted black bears this inscription: "This is the place of Marino Paliero, beheaded for his crimes (1336)." "Crime" is an ugly companion to a name in an epitaph! But the meaning of the word is relative. The loftiest virtue in one land is sometimes crime in another. In Venice, in the fourteenth century, a revolt against the tyranny of the Council of Ten was treason and the blackest crime. When Faliero, who had brilliantly served Venice in foreign lands all his life, was recalled from Avignon, where he was Ambassador at the Court of the Pope, to fill the office of Doge, and when the ducal cap, with its circlet of gold, was placed upon his head, and the ducal ring upon his finger, he believed he was receiving the crowning reward for a life-long devotion to the state. But when he found that he was a mere lay-figure in humiliating bondage to that secret tribunal, in the hands of younger men, and when he received taunts and slights and insult from those who should have trembled in his presence, his indignant fury seemed to turn his brain. An insane impulse seized him to overthrow the whole odious tyranny which was ruining his city. It ended as we have seen. The old man met his doom at the head of the stairs in the Ducal Palace, and there the empty panel has proclaimed his disgrace ever since. But it might be a grim satisfaction to the proud old Venetian could he know that, for that very reason, his name among the other seventy-six Doges is almost the only one the world will never forget! One other, the name Foscari, has also attained a tragic immortality; Francesco Foscari, after wearing the ducal cap for a number of years, was compelled by the Council of Ten to preside over the torture of his only son. The obdurate tribunal refusing to receive his resignation, and insisting upon the unproved guilt of the young man, three times compelled him to sit in the torture-chamber and see his adored son broken to pieces upon the rack. All this he heroically bore. But when the Council tried to disgrace him by taking the ducal ring from his finger and breaking it in pieces, and then drove him from the Palace, the old man's heart broke, and he died as the bells were ringing in his successor (1425). Then they bore him back to the Palace from which they had just expelled him, placed the ducal cap again on his dead brow, gave him the most magnificent funeral the Republic could bestow, and covered him with sculptured marble in the Church of the Frari.

The city of Milan, already populous and powerful, was now taking on a new splendor which would make her forever great in the architectural world. Her matchless cathedral, with its wilderness of statues, was in process of erection. Cimabue and Giotto and their followers had for almost a century been making Florence beautiful, and laying the foundations of the Italian school of painting. Those delicate flowers, poesy and art, with their strange tendency to adorn rough and unlovely places with their tender grace, were beginning to weave a filmy delicate mantle over Italy. While that awful pestilence, the Black Death, was stalking over the land, Boccaccio wrote his

Decameron, and was reciting its hundred stories for the diversion of panic-stricken Florentines (1347 A.D.). And in the midst of distracting political agitations, with the earth perpetually trembling beneath his feet in Rome and in Florence (1304-74), Petrarch, proudly wearing the laureate's crown, was writing sonnets and striving to create a new intellectual life by infusing into the people his own passionate ardor for the literature of past ages, and was thus sowing the first seeds for a coming Renaissance.

The prolonged absence from Rome had greatly impaired the dignity and the authority of the Church, but in spite of protests and entreaties the popes still lingered in France. Its remoteness from the perpetual agitations at Rome, its luxurious repose and isolation, made Avignon a fascinating abode to the cardinals, who resisted all attempts to re-establish the papal residence in the Eternal City. But in 1367, Pope Gregory XI., moved by the prayers of a saintly woman, St. Catharine of Siena, went to Rome and survived the change just one year. There then commenced a disgraceful quarrel between popes and cardinals which lasted for half a century. The cardinals, under the guidance of the Holy Spirit, had placed Urban VI in the vacant chair at Rome. But when they discovered that he was arrogant, domineering, and intractable, and perhaps—that he would not return to Avignon they also discovered that the Holy Spirit had this time made a mistake. They repudiated him and elected another— Clement VII. So now there were two infallible popes, one at Rome and another at Avignon, each claiming universal dominion by virtue of his being the one and only vicegerent of Christ upon earth. While the air was vibrating with anathemas and excommunications hurled from Rome to Avignon, and from Avignon back again to Borne, a church council was called which took upon itself the settlement of the dispute by deposing both popes, and electing another under the title of Alexander V. So now there were three infallible and only vicars of Christ reigning over His kingdom upon earth, and Europe was divided in allegiance, its conscience confused, and its religious enthusiasm chilled. This is known as "the great Schism of the West." Not until the fifteenth century was the disgraceful breach healed, when, at the church council at Constance in 1414, all three popes were formally deposed and Martin V., a prince of the great house of Colonna, was solemnly placed in the papal chair at Rome.

The important point established by the action of this council was, not that Martin V was the rightful Pope, but that the supreme ecclesiastical power was vested in the council; and that the decisions of a collective episcopate, composed of prelates from all the Catholic states of Europe, was the court of last appeal to which even popes must bow; a limitation of papal prerogative which would have been startling to Gregory VII, or to Innocent III when he was deposing kings in England and in France, and claiming an authority with no visible frontier. But this was only a spasmodic reform, as later events showed.

In the south of Italy at this time a young queen was on the throne of Naples, whose troubled life-story bears some curious points of resemblance to that of Mary Queen of Scots two hundred years later. While only a child of sixteen, she was a queen, and already married to her cousin, who was making himself odious by insisting that he should share her authority. This troublesome consort was one day invited into an upper chamber, a silken noose was deftly thrown about his neck, and he was pushed out of the window. Then, before the clamor over his murder had died away, the beautiful Joanna was wedded to the man believed to be the chief instigator of the plot. Interest in this romance is enhanced by the knowledge that Boccaccio was one of the fascinating Queen's many adorers, and warmly championed her during her stormy career, which was tragically ended in 1383, by her being smothered by pillows in her bed.

As the fourteenth century was closing, the popes were ruling at Rome. In the south the Angevines were holding a luxurious and voluptuous court at Naples, and the Arragonese were reigning in Sicily. In the north, Milan was grasping all within her reach, and Florence beginning to tremble before her, she herself being engaged the while in humbling beautiful and brave Pisa. Genoa's star was declining, while Venice sat triumphant upon her throne on the shining Adriatic.

There had been wars, and desolation, and pestilence, and tumultuous changes at every point—no rest, no repose. And yet a country which in one century had been given a Dante, a Giotto, a Petrarch, and a Boccaccio, had not been entirely forgotten by the gods!

Chapter VI

In this story of Italy a name destined more than any other to shape her ultimate future has not yet been heard. Lying in the sun under the shadow of the Alps, and back from the sea in safe, noiseless obscurity, was the little province of Savoy. Possessing nothing that others wanted, and with no extravagant outreaching desires of its own, this bit of territory had been quietly expanding since the beginning of the eleventh century, when a certain Humbert, a German count, obtained it as a gift from the Duke of Burgundy. By judicious marriages, and by gradual encroachments upon his neighbors, the tract had expanded into quite a large state, and in 1388 the province of Nice, lying between it and the sea, needing protection from French encroachments, voluntarily annexed herself to her sturdy mountaineer neighbor in the north, and so to the realm of mountains, and forest, and ravines, was now added a much-needed line of seacoast. The state of Savoy had thus at once become important, and a factor in the affairs of the peninsula. So in the year 1413 the Emperor Sigismund dignified the territory with the name of duchy, and Count Amadeus VIII., the descendant of the first Humbert, became Duke of Savoy, the new duchy of course becoming a fief of the empire. Duke Amadeus, realizing the peril of his position in being so near to the grasping Duke of Milan, at once formed an alliance with Florence and Venice which was mutually advantageous, and from this time the dukes of Savoy, the "janitors of the Alps," as they have been called, appear, disappear, and reappear again with telling effect in the story of Italy. Upon the deposition of Eugenius IV., Duke Amadeus was offered the papal chair with the title Felix V. He abdicated his dukedom in favor of his son and reigned over the pontificate for a brief period, then prudently resigned in favor of a more popular candidate. In proof of the high esteem in which he was held, he was always thereafter permitted to wear a part of the pontifical dress, and had the special privilege of giving the Pope a fraternal kiss upon the cheek, instead of kissing his toe.

All of which is interesting as evidence of the ability and adroitness which distinguished the first Duke of Savoy.

During the last century another complicating network of circumstances had been spun over Italy. Bands of adventurers had swarmed into the peninsula from other lands, offering to fight the battles of anyone who would pay for their service. Known as free lances in other countries, these in Italy were called *condottieri*. What had at first been a disorderly vagrant host, plundering right and left, had now become a regularly organized system of merce-naries. Wars were incessant, and were an interruption to industry and hence to prosperity, something dearer than aught else to the Italian cities. By em-ploying the condottieri, the merchant princes in Florence, and Venice, and Milan, need have no conscription arresting peaceful pursuits, and might still go on piling up riches, while their paid servants fought their battles. The story of Carmagnola shows to what heights these soldiers of fortune might climb, and to what depths they might also fall. A rustic from the mountains of Piedmont, Carmagnola, while only a boy, joined the condottieri. His ge-nius for military affairs advanced him rapidly, and early in the fifteenth century he was the commander-in-chief of the Milanese army. When the stern old conquering Duke Gian Galeazzo died, and the smaller Lombard cities, Parma, Cremona, Lodi, Piacenza, struggled out of the grasp of his son Philip, he it was who brought them back into subjection and made Milan stronger than before. So now the Piedmontese peasant was a great general, and the terror of Florentines and Venetians, and of all the enemies of Milan. For his reward he was given a Visconti for his bride, and dwelt in a palace, and was treated as a prince. This awoke envy, and ways of undermining him ware discovered. The Duke's attitude toward him suddenly changed. His feelings wounded, stung to madness by a sense of ingratitude, in a sudden access of rage Carmagnola turned his back upon Milan and rode across the frontier into Savoy. There he offered his services to Duke Amadeus, his na-tive prince, suggesting ways in which he could extend his frontier on the side toward Milan! But the Duke was too prudent to accept the opportunity, and Carmagnola then presented himself before the Senate in Venice with a similar offer. Who so well as he knew the strength and the weakness of their terrible enemy, Milan.

Nothing better could have come to Venice at this time while in league with Florence and Savoy against the terrible power in the north. She hated Florence only a little less than Milan, and would not have been displeased to leave her to her fate. So the great condottiere was invested with absolute authority and lived again in a palace and like a prince, basking in the friend-ship of the Doge, Francesco Foscari, he also not yet under the shadow of tragedy! And there were many victories, and Duke Philip of Milan saw his armies destroyed by the general whose strategy and invincibility he so well knew. But the time came when in a struggle over Cremona there was a crushing defeat for the Venetians, Carmagnola said because his advice had not been followed. There were no reproaches. Carmagnola, on the contrary, was assured by the Senate of their continued confidence might he not some day ride back to Milan in the same way he had come to them. A flattering invitation came for him to return to Venice for a conference with the "Most

Serene Prince and the illustrious Senators." When he arrived he was conducted by his courtier-attendants directly to the Doge's Palace. He was led through a labyrinth of halls, growing dimmer and dimmer, until a door was opened and he realized his fate— he was in a dungeon. The fatal doors were only to open again as he passed from day to day to the torture-chamber, where in the presence of the Secret Council it was expected to wring from him a confession of having betrayed them at Cremona to the Duke of Milan. Whether the month of torture accomplished this, no one knew. It is only known that on May 5, 1432, the great chief was led out, with his mouth gagged, to his execution on the plaza. In this way was justice administered in beautiful Venice. Perhaps when the aged and stricken Doge was witnessing his own son's tortures, not long after, he may have recalled Carmagnola and the "torture-chamber," and the last scene "between the columns."

But the defeat at Cremona so fatal to Carmagnola made the fortune of another great condottiere, Francesco Sforza's star steadily rose after that day in 1431, when he was the victorious general in command of the Milanese army, and when Duke Philip died without an heir and there was no Visconti to succeed him, the brilliant soldier of fortune, as commander-in-chief, controlled the situation. By finesse and by audacity he seized the vacant throne and planted the dynasty of the Sforzas (1450). This usurper, who ruled wisely for those times, was the grandson of a peasant, but claimed descent from a person no less distinguished than Porsenna, King of Etruria, the champion of the exiled King Tarquin! The genius for statecraft and the soaring ambition of this man prepared the way for the line of dukes which was to follow him. They had not the wolf-like qualities of the Viscontis, did not find entertainment in hunting their peasants with bloodhounds, but with more refined methods, while a little less cruel, proved more dangerous to Italy.

Chapter VII

In Florence a new family had come into control of the Republic. The name dei Medici indicates that their ancestors had been members of one of the ancient city guilds—not necessarily as practising the profession of medicine, but as a qualification for participating in the government. By mercantile pursuits this family had amassed great wealth, and by lavish liberality and integrity and by intelligence had acquired popularity and influence. Cosimo de' Medici (1389-1404 A.D.), the son of a long line of merchants, by his talent for administration and his affability, and by his princely generosity, had attained the position of an untitled prince. His power became almost supreme. Whom he would he raised, and whom he would he abased. Of course the ruling oligarchy was jealous and tried to destroy him. He was accused, it mattered little of what, banished, and then recalled triumphant, because they could not get along without his sustaining and guiding hand, which kept the people in the path of peace, prosperity and wealth. He gathered about him great artists, commissioned Branelleschi to complete the plans for the Duomo, and employed Ghiberti, Donatello and Luca della Robbia to adorn buildings with their matchless sculptures. In this founder of the house of Medici, we see all the traits which so distinguished this epoch-making family,—the passion for learning and for art and for all that makes for supreme culture and intellectual refinement, and joined to this that subtle quality which made him the despotic master of the people without their knowing it. The friend of the democracy and its munificent benefactor, what more could they ask? Holding no office, no title, be left to his descendants a legacy of power, a firm grasp upon the state which it would not find easy to shake off.

In 1453 an event of transcendent importance occurred. The capture of Constantinople by the Turks thrilled Europe with a tide of new intellectual life. Greek scholars and Greek literature carried into every land the thought and the ideals of the great past.

The Turks in freeing these hoarded treasures were the unconscious benefactors of Europe, and Christendom while weeping for Constantinople was just as unconsciously enriched by its loss. But for Italy a Renaissance had been in progress for a century. A passion for ancient Greek manuscripts, and for Greek culture and ideals, was not new; it had existed since Petrarch taught the Colonnas the subtle charm of these things. And Florence was already instinct with the spirit of the Renaissance when its transforming tide swept over the rest of Europe. So, as was natural, it was the Florentines who were the most influential in guiding this new impulse, and it was the Medicean family which stood at the gateway between the old and the new culture.

It was Lorenzo de' Medici, the grandson of Cosimo, who gave the final impress to the character of the Medicean policy. Florence was to be a personal despotism, and he, its magnificent ruler and patron. His own fortune was great, but not great enough to carry out his princely designs, so he drew upon the public treasury. Here was an opportunity for his downfall, which was carefully planned by the Pope and a family of jealous Florentine nobles — the Pazzis. By a preconcerted plot he and his brother, while at high mass in the Duomo, were attacked by assassins. His brother was slain, but Lorenzo survived to witness the effacement of the Pazzi family by the enraged Florentines, and his own exaltation far beyond what it had been before the conspiracy. A hideous fringe of dead conspirators hung from the windows of the Signoria, an archbishop and two priests were among the slain, and the people were not appeased until the last of the enemies of their benefactor had been slaughtered. Pope Sixtus IV enlisted the King of Naples to aid in avenging the death of his archbishop. But the persuasive and wily Lorenzo went himself to Naples and in one interview induced the King to abandon his purpose, cunningly showing him how much more advantageous would be the friendship of Florence than her enmity. Then, this diplomatic triumph accomplished, Lorenzo returned to bury out of sight the liberties of the republic by converting the elective body of the state into a permanent council appointed by himself. It was a delightful enslavement. Their city, like a second Athens, was growing splendid and drawing to itself the learning and culture and art of all Italy. It had Michel Angelo, the greatest genius that ever wrought in marble, to sculpture its monuments and to adorn its walls, and Ghirlandajo and Ghiberti and della Robbia to embellish its palaces. The age of Pericles had come again. They still exulted in the name of Republic, and so lightly did their chains rest upon them, that they believed they were free!

But beneath these splendid refinements, and the scholarship and the fastidious taste and breeding, there was a morass of wickedness. Religion and morality, as we understand them, did not exist, nor did nobility of character, nor truth, nor honor, nor even decency in the conduct of life. Yet Florence, selfish, sordid, sensual, was chosen for the strangest outpouring of genius that, with a single exception, ever came to one city. Brunelleschi, Ghiberti, Ghirlandajo, Angelico, Robbia, Leonardo, Raphael and Michel Angelo,—such is a partial list of the names enrolled in one century—a century of incredible corruption and a climax in the moral degradation of Italy!

What are we to think of the magnificent patron of a new culture who writes ribald songs and choruses for the people to sing upon the streets? and what of the people who take pleasure in these things? One asks in bewilderment whether the putrid elements of decomposing character are what genius feeds upon. And whether it be true that art and spiritual elevation are antagonistic, and that art and morals must dwell in different realms! However this may be, Florence under Lorenzo "the Magnificent" reached the sublimest heights in art, and a perfection of aesthetic development which was to be a model for the world—and yet she was base.

Italy's moral condition at this time is like the negative of a photograph. It precisely reverses the standards of today. It makes highlights of shadows, and shadows of highlights. What they called virtuous we consider infamous. What to us is essential to decency of character, to them would have been compromising, and even fatal to social or political reputation. The standing of a man was not injured by his being considered vicious or perfidious, but nothing could be worse than a reputation for simplicity! One might lie and use fraud and deception, but to be incapable, or to sin against taste—these were crimes for which no genius would atone.

In the evolution of the Italian republics not one elevating influence had been at work. Intensely narrow in their patriotism, the well-being of each state demanded the destruction of the rest. The prosperity of Florence required that she should sap the life of Pisa, and that of Venice, that she should destroy her competitor Genoa, and Milan, that she should devour all within her reach. A policy so debasing to national character would have extinguished native nobility had it existed. Instead of wisely drawing together for mutual protection and advantage, they were always driven apart by fierce antagonisms. Italy was in fact a disintegrated mass held together by perfectly artificial systems needing only a touch from a more firmly compacted body to fall into ruin. She was not an organism, but an ingenious mechanism. Nothing had developed from a life principle within; all was artificially imposed from without, and was held together by that vicious combination of fraud, violence, and subtle wickedness, called statecraft.

The source of the poison which was coursing in the veins of Italy was the Papal Kingdom. When an open profligate could buy the suffrages of the cardinals and become the primate of Christendom, and when he could publicly acknowledge his illegitimate sons and daughters, could set his price upon sin, and then for his own enrichment establish an organized system for the sale of pardons, how could virtue exist in the land? This is what Innocent III was doing, his traffic in crime having, it is said, filled the Campagna with brigands and assassins. Religion, instead of a renovating, purifying, spiritual influence, had become simply a system by which men might placate a wrathful God by gifts, and if these were frequent and rich enough, they might sin to the bent of their desires. It was for revolt against such a church as this that the Inquisition was torturing and burning heretics, and that John Huss and Jerome of Prague had suffered martyrdom, and that the Walden sea were to be slaughtered like sheep in the shambles!

But good breeding and taste demanded. that the Church be sustained, and nowhere in Italy was the martyr's crown in great request. The mental energies of Italy were fully occupied with the Renaissance. Florence had a great work in hand. She was laying the foundations of modern culture. It would be too much to expect that she should at the same time be conducting a spiritual reformation. She had her own mission, and was performing it with supreme excellence, and if under the despotic sway of Lorenzo, that magnificent pagan, she was being emancipated somewhat from the Church which had excommunicated her on his account, we are compelled to think that paganism was not a bad exchange for a religion which had become so depraved and so debasing to the conscience of its children. But the truth pure and undefiled still existed; not in the hierarchy, not at Rome, but in the deep recesses of human hearts. In Italy and everywhere were men and women in whose souls the sacred flame was burning with undiminished ardor, and untarnished purity, and this it was which brought the living waters safely through the centuries, and through the unspeakable defilements of ecclesiasticism:

There was one such soul now in Italy struggling with the problem of sin. Savonarola, a Dominican friar born in Ferrara, had from his childhood been oppressed with a sense of the sinfulness of Italy. Sent to preach to the Florentines, he found their city given up to sensual pleasures. Under the influence of its splendid tyrant, the worship of beauty and of pagan culture was its religion. He tried to tell them of their peril, but it was the voice of one crying in the wilderness. It was Lorenzo de' Medici, the man who had taken away their liberties, he it was who had thus perverted their hearts with paganism! If Florence was to be saved he must be destroyed. A warning voice within gave him no peace; night and day it said, "Cry aloud and spare not." He seemed to be taken possession of by something not of himself, and the spirit of prophecy came upon him. He saw a foreign host sweeping through the land, Italy ravaged, and blood flowing in the streets of Florence, and then a purified Church rising over a penitent and stricken Italy. In visions and in trances again and again he saw these things. He must tell the people of their coming doom. "Repent—repent— while there is yet time!" That was the burden of his cry. Crowds began to throng the Duomo to catch the rushing torrent of his words. He laid bare the wickedness of their hearts and the iniquity of their lives with such an unsparing hand that men trembled and women cried aloud in terror. A scribe who preserved portions of these sermons breaks off in his narrative with these words, "Here I was so overcome with weeping that I could not go on." Another one says, "His words caused such terror, alarm, sobbing and tears that everyone passed out into the streets without speaking, more dead than alive."

Lorenzo, wishing the best of everything for Florence, was pleased to have the great preacher remain. Perhaps it touched his aesthetic sense to listen to his strange inspired eloquence, like a prophet of old, and to watch that austere, haggard face, with the deep-set eyes, burning and flashing from beneath his cowl. But when the darts began to strike him, when the preacher would not meet him, because he was the enemy of Florence, then his feelings changed. Perfectly antagonistic, these men represented hostile principles. But the paganism of which Lorenzo was the incarnation, was quite as much a revolt against a corrupt church as was Savonarola's dream of a new spiritual baptism, and it was intended in the evolutionary process to accomplish the spiritual resurrection he sought, not by methods such as the "impassioned reformer would have chosen, but by the emancipation of human thought from the trammels he venerated and upheld. The great preacher, inspired seer though he was, did not understand the solution of the problem. The Renaissance was a necessary highway in human progress which led directly to Luther.

Still another mind different in quality from both of these was in Florence at this time, forecasting the future, and pointing out the path of safety. Righteousness was not upon his banner, nor did he call upon people to "repent." This was Machiavelli, statesman, cynic, and philosopher. His acute mind grasped the idea of unity as the hope of Italy, and also clearly traced the corruption and prevailing disunion to the Church as its source. The Church must be held subordinate in the state, rivalries and antagonisms must cease, and all must come under one prince—that prince to be Lorenzo de Medici. Such was the plan outlined in his famous work The Prince—the most sagacious and at the same time the most audacious and infamous book ever given to the world. Dedicated to Lorenzo, it is intended as a hand-book for princes—showing how to acquire power, and how to keep it. It measures with scientific accuracy the amount of cruelty needed under different conditions to make a city helpless. In speaking of free cities, in view of the troublesome vitality in the idea of liberty, he says—"to speak the truth, the only safe way, is to ruin them." Men may sometimes be managed by caressing; if not, they should "be trampled out." He sneers at Baglioni, because he had not the courage to strangle his guest, Julius II., after dinner. The only despicable quality is weakness. So with refreshing frankness he proceeds to lay bare Italian political methods. Everyone knew that such were the means used by the Venetian Council, and the Papal Court, and the Sforzas, but that it should be calmly and philosophically stated, that duplicity and fraud and cold-blooded cruelty were the proper path to power, and the essential weapons after it was acquired—this it is which has astonished the world for five centuries! The corrupting influence of The Prince upon France and Spain at the time is undoubted, and we are not surprised to hear that the Spanish princes and the sons of Catharine de Medici were at a later period careful students of this manual of political crime. Machiavelli's strictures upon the Church sound like Satan reproving sin. But while he must have admired the Christian hierarchy as the finest specimen of his art, yet viewed in its relation to the political condition of Italy, he disapproved of it, because he had the wisdom to see that the hope of Italy lay in making the Church subordinate to a central authority. Savonarola, on the other hand, thinking only of righteousness and attacking the sins of the Pope as fiercely as those of the people, would have thought it impious to impair the authority of the Church, or alter its structure one iota.

The day came when Lorenzo needed the preacher. He was dying, and sent to Savonarola to come and open the door of Heaven for him by the sacraments of the Church, and by absolution. He would have none but the Dominican, for none other was honest. The friar, standing by the dying man, required three things as the condition for absolving him. He must throw himself upon God's mercy, which he was willing to do; mast restore all property unjustly acquired, to which he also consented; and he must give Florence back her liberty! The friar had asked too much of the dying sinner with only minutes to live. He silently turned his face to the wall, and died unshriven.

Chapter VIII

The year of Lorenzo's death, 1492, was great in the world's chronology. It witnessed the expulsion of the Moors from Granada, and the final triumph of Spain after her struggle of 700 years. It saw the European states, every one, held under the dominion of a strong centralized authority which had forever effaced feudalism. But greater than all else, another world was revealed, beyond the mysterious Western Ocean. The full significance of this was not suspected; but Queen Isabella's gold, and kindness, and proselyting spirit had forged the most important link in the chain of circumstances since the birth of Christ. Then, as always, however, the emphasis was placed upon events which would become invisible through the perspective of centuries. The death of Lorenzo and of the reigning Pope seemed vastly more important than the discovery made by the Genoese. Who would wear the tiara, was the all-absorbing question. It was a great opportunity for the cardinals. They had bought their red hats with gold, and now might get the price back by selling their suffrages! Roderigo Borgia, from Valencia, Spain, was the richest, wisest, and most cunning of the candidates. He knew the price of every one of the conclave: that Cardinal Sforza, brother of the Duke of Milan, wanted to be Vice Chancellor; that Cardinal Orsini had long had his eye upon the Borgia palaces in Rome; that while Cardinal Colonna preferred the Abbey of Subiaco with its fortresses, another thirsted for the Bishopric of Porto, with its palace and well-stocked wine-cellars; others again being satisfied with gold. And so it was that in 1492 the mantle of St. Peter was placed upon Roderigo Borgia, who assumed the title Alexander VI. The reign of Nero among the emperors was not a greater climax than this first Borgia's among the popes. No less sensual, no less grasping of power than Nero, he claimed an unlimited authority—which even included the hemisphere just discovered by Columbus, which he generously divided between Spain and Portugal—and also just as unlimited indulgence in his own private and personal life.

His hand was strong, and guided by craft and sagacity. So his first work was to humble the great princes—and to destroy the faction between Colonnas and Orsinis. So active was the sale of indulgences and pardons that an epigram then current says: "Alexander sells the keys, the altars, and Christ. Well—he bought them, so has he not the right to sell them!" But if he gave a heavy price for his tiara, he cunningly got it back in creating forty-three new cardinals, each of whom paid him a fortune for his hat. Twelve of these, it is said, were sold at auction in one day.

The one man he could not buy was Savonarola. He tried it with honeyed words and blandishments, offering him a cardinal's hat if he would come to Rome. But the friar replied that he preferred the red crown of martyrdom. A crusade against sin was not pleasant to a pope steeped in crime and profligacy, who was showering benefits upon his illegitimate children, making Cesar Borgia at eighteen a cardinal, and contracting a royal alliance for his daughter Lucrezia. He could easily have silenced the voice of the preacher at Rome, but as the friar would not walk into his trap, he suspended him.

Savonarola had struck a new note in his inspired declamation. He was the champion of liberty. Political freedom was inseparable from righteousness, and, like Ezekiel and Jeremiah and Jonah and all the prophets of old, he believed it was his mission to overthrow tyranny and to destroy wicked rulers and constitutions. So, without ceasing, he incited the people to cast off the rule of the Medici, which had descended to Piero, the feeble son of Lorenzo.

Ludovico Sforza for his own purposes invited Charles VIII., King of France, to invade Italy with the purpose of establishing a shadowy claim upon Naples, offering the assistance of Lombardy in the enterprise. And in 1494 Savonarola's prophecy was fulfilled. A French army entering by the territories of the Duke of Milan, marched southward, and achieved a bloodless triumph over Italy. Florence and Rome, without resistance, were handed over to him by Piero de Medici and Alexander VI. After proclaiming himself King of Naples, Charles returned to France, and Italy, except for the humiliation, and the discovery of her weakness by Europe remained much as before.

Savonarola's words had been verified! The excited Florentines believing he alone could save them, he became practically a dictator. Piero and his house were driven out, and the preacher planned a new constitution for a new Florence. A spiritual madness seized the people. Instead of vile songs, hymns were sung upon the streets, and young and old pledged themselves to lives of piety and austerity. A day was appointed for the burning of vanities, when there was a great holocaust of finery and adornments and books; Boccaccio, and the classic poets, and MSS., and rare paintings were given to the flames. It was a revival—the greatest the world ever saw. It was Puritanism run mad in Florence! This was the climax. The burning of works of art, the insult to the new culture, roused the fury of its adherents. They joined hands with the Pope to destroy this prophet of evil who was holding Florence in his hand. A reaction from the tense emotional strain also came, and when the city was under an interdict by the Pope, and no sacraments could be administered for the living or rites for the dead, some of Savonarola's followers fell away from him. The ordeal by fire was proposed to learn whether or no he really was of God, as he claimed. The furnace was prepared, the Franciscan who had offered to join him in the test was ready, and the people assembled to witness a miracle. But Savonarola did not come— and at last a heavy rain extinguished the fires. The faith of the people was shaken, and a prison (in the tower of the Signoria Palace) closed upon the fallen dictator. There are vague rumors of prolonged tortures, and of confessions and retractions shrieked by him while in the delirium of the rack. How much is true no one knows—only that on the 23d of May, 1898, he came before the people for the last time. As the fires were lighted beneath him, and the noose adjusted about his neck, a jeering voice cried, "Prophet—now is the time for a miracle!" The only words he uttered were, "The Lord has suffered as much for me,"—and the rope and the fire did their work.

The French invasion by Charles, barren of immediate results, was the showy prelude to the real performance. It was the noisy, harmless shower preceding the deluge. Europe had found out that Italy was an easy prey for any adventurous kingdom. But there was a still deeper cause for the overturnings which were at hand. In the path of progress Europe had moved from the rule of many masters into the strong keeping of four or five. Feudalism was dead. Diversity had had its day and accomplished its work, and the hour had struck for unity. Europe contained a group of firmly compacted absolutisms, each despotically governed by a central authority, and all bound together again into a larger unity by diplomatic threads. What was done by Ferdinand and Isabella in Spain, thrilled the Court of Maximilian at Vienna; every move of England and France in like manner vibrated through the entire group of despotisms. A tide bearing the principle of unity, had moved over the face of Europe, even Russia, remote and separated, keeping step with the general advance. Italy alone was left behind, and in a Europe ruled by kings and parliaments there lingered five mediaeval states, with dukes and doges, and gonfaloniers, and signorias, and grand councils, all crowded together in a small area, upon a small peninsula. Engaged in deadly rivalry with one another, they were playing an antiquated game upon an absurdly small field. They were an anachronism in Europe. That the wave should sweep over them was just as inevitable as that the tide should cover a low-lying strip of land. It might be as surely prophesied as that the sun should rise after the dawn. The intellectual awakening of the Renaissance, so hateful to Savonarola, was the first streak of light in the dawn of the new day—a day which would reach its high noon when not alone the intellect but the conscience was emancipated, and when men had learned to know the height, the depth, and the breadth of the word—liberty! The discovery of new sources of wealth in the West, the diverting of the trade energies from the old Eastern highways, this and all the circumstances pointing to the downfall of the proud mediaeval republics, were only acting under a more comprehensive law of progress, which majestically moves on its appointed way through the centuries. The republics had lost their golden opportunity; and since they would not conform to the prevailing spirit, would not of their own will combine, and centralize, they were to be ground in the mills of the gods for three centuries, until they were fused, every trace of the old rigid landmarks obliterated, and Italy prepared to be a homogeneous nation.

In 1499 a new energetic king, Louis of France, invaded the peninsula, in alliance, not with the intriguing Duke of Milan, but with Ferdinand, the King of Naples, with whom he was to divide the spoil, the Pope consenting to the unholy league. The work was quickly accomplished, and then the crafty Spaniard took all the fruits of the victory for himself, and ruled Naples and Sicily under one crown. The aggrieved Louis turned to the Emperor Maximilian. They formed an alliance to subjugate Venice, Louis seemingly unconscious that a Charles V. was soon coming on the stage, who would be joint heir to the German Empire and Spain, and the overwhelming rival of France. So by 1516 Spain, France, and Germany were trampling over the soil of Italy, the infatuated states the while pursuing their petty animosities just as before, each still thinking only of its own peril or advantage, Alexander VI., the Infamous, had died by a cup of poison which it is said he and his son Cesar had prepared for some troublesome cardinals. This may not be true. But one crime more or less makes little difference in the record left by Cesar Borgia, which has probably not been exceeded even in Italy. He it is who is held up by Machiavelli as the perfect specimen of the art of state-craft. It was Cesar Borgia alone who satisfied the artistic sense of this fastidious anatomist of political villainy. With no vulgar impulsiveness, with perfect self-command, he could be deliberately cruel with definite ends in view. With a steady hand he could assassinate his brother, or strangle a group of friends, not because he disliked them, but because they were an obstruction. It was the splendid intelligence of his cruelty which charmed Machiavelli, the supreme subtlety with which he established himself in the seat his father carved out for him, and played his game for power with Spain and with France, by bribes and promises, and perfidy within perfidy, meeting every obstruction, not with coarse violence, but with quiet stranglings, and poison, which he would compel his agents to administer for him, and then execute them for the crime with a show of indignation. His cruelty was never purposeless, but intended to terrify and thus to subjugate. There was this intention even in that famous incident, when he entertained his father and sister Lucrezia for an afternoon by shooting arrows at condemned criminals brought into the court of the palace for that purpose. He knew the temper of the Italian people, and that terror accomplished more than blandishments, and in anticipation of his father's death, he was firmly establish-establishing himself in his new territory.

Such was the man held up by a sagacious Florentine patriot as a model for the imitation of Lorenzo, in ruling a republic.

Alexander VI. was succeeded by Julius II., a man with fewer vices and larger ambitions. At first favoring the alliance against Venice, he became alarmed for his own kingdom, and conceived a plan of a federation of all the Italian states, which should then be ruled by his own progeny. With important European powers he formed a Holy League, for the expulsion of the French and Germans, which led to the battle of Ravenna (1512).

Julius is best remembered as a patron of art. He it was who created the Vatican museum. The Apollo of the Belvidere bad been recently unearthed, and also the Laocoon had just been found buried beneath the Baths of Titus. He employed Bramante to lay the foundations of St. Peter's at Rome, and then Raphael and Michel Angelo to continue the work. It is his connection with the incomparable masterpieces of these two men which invests the name of Julius with interest. Michel Angelo's "Moses" was one of the figures created for his monument. Leo X., who succeeded Julius in 1513, was one of the Medici family. He immediately employed the great sculptor to design and decorate the chapel of the Medici at Florence, where he had re-established the authority of his family. It was in fulfilment of this commission that the great work commemorative of Lorenzo de Medici in that city was executed.

The building of St. Peter's, the magnificent plans for its embellishment, the decorating of the Sistine Chapel of the Vatican, and other art projects, required a great deal of money, more than Leo could command. So he proclaimed a sale of special indulgences and sent his messengers into Germany to collect the golden stream which was sure to come from this traffic in sin and crime.

Martin Luther, originally a monk, but then a professor in the University at Wittenberg, already burning with indignation at the impurities of the Church, wrote a stinging denunciation of this last infamy, which he nailed upon the door of the old Castle Church (1617). This seemed a small matter at Rome, but it was going to shake the Church to its centre. The smothered fires burst into an uncontrollable conflagration, and Europe was convulsed with the Reformation.

While Protestantism was overturning Europe and wearing out the heart of the overburdened Charles V., in Germany, it made little difference in Italy. Charles, the grandson of Isabella and Ferdinand, and also of Maximilian, in 1519 bore the weight of two crowns, his power extending over two hemispheres. He determined to settle matters in Italy. He received his Imperial crown from the Pope, then as their master summoned the Italian princes to meet him at Milan. Florence was secured to the Medici, who were to rule under the title of Dukes of Florence. A Spanish viceroy was placed at Milan, and another in Naples, and the whole peninsula was left in a condition of inglorious servitude to his agents.

Chapter IX

From 1530 to 1796 Italy has no history of its own. Would you know its perturbations and overturnings during three centuries, you must look for them in the histories of Spain, France, and Germany. It was the battleground for alien armies fighting over issues with which it had nothing to do, the people driven like dumb cattle before Hapsburgs and Bourbons and drinking the cup of humiliation to the dregs. Francis I. and Charles V. fought out their long battle on Italian soil. When Francis was taken prisoner and carried to Spain, and the army of Charles had possession, scaling ladders were planted against the walls of Rome (1527 A.D.), and again was that city the scene of horror, ravaged by a German mob, the Pope hiding in the castle of St. Angelo, while the worst passions of a ferocious and brutal army were let loose upon the inhabitants, rivalling in horror the sacking by Goths and Vandals. After this came another Medicean Pope, Clement VII., he who drove Henry VIII. into Protestantism by his indecision over the matter of the divorce, Catharine, the wife Henry wished to repudiate, being the aunt of Charles V, whom he must not offend.

Again did the Florentines attempt a republic, this time under a gonfalonier appointed for life, and again were the Medicis driven out. Catharine, grand-daughter of Piero, son of Lorenzo, was the wife of the Dauphin of France, who upon the death of Francis I would be Henry II. Until this intriguing family in alliance with despotism was expelled, there could be no liberty for Florence, so once more the city was closed upon them, only to see them soon return again as Grand Dukes of Tuscany, more powerful than ever. It was in 1580 that one of these sumptuous Grand Dukes gave to Vasari the commission to build the gallery which connects the Uffizi and Pitti palaces.

All this concerns sovereigns and pontiffs and princes. Of the people there is little to say except that wretchedness reigned. The plains once fertile and blooming were a desert—prosperity was destroyed and towns depopulated. The attempt of Genoa to establish a republic under Andrew Dona, a son of one of her ancient families, in 1628, was not unsuccessful. It continued in force until the French Revolution. Of just such unrelated fragments as these does the history of this period consist. Nothing that happens seems connected with what precedes nor what succeeds it. Things done are just as speedily undone, the changes in the shifting scene being no more significant than those made by the turning of a kaleidoscope. It is a story of ineffectual popes striving to cope with a deluge, and to reinforce the crumbling foundations of the Church; and of waning cities trying to hide their decay, and to keep up the semblance of their ancient glories. The order of Jesuits was founded, and the Council of Trent solemnly proclaimed a statement of Catholic doctrine, intended to reform and yet to strengthen the authority of the popes, and the foundations of the venerated structure. After the abdication of Charles V. came the reign of his son, Philip II, the champion of the faith, reinvigorating the assaults upon Protestantism in his own remorseless fashion, with his efficient aid, the Duke of Alva.

The pontificate of Gregory XIII. (1572-86 A.D.) is marked by the reform in the calendar which was finally adopted by all of Christendom, except where the Greek Church prevailed, so that today Russia and Greece are twelve days in advance of the rest of Europe. This was the period of the religious wars in France, which were terminated when Henry IV. was received into the Church by Clement VIII. Pope Clement is also remembered in connection with the burning, for alleged heresy, of Giordano Bruno, the most learned and distinguished scholar of his age; and also with the torture and death of Beatrice Cenci, for the crime of parricide—an act which, although deserved, was never proved.

The Duchy of Savoy, remote and unobserved, continued to grow. Her dukes, by ambitious marriages and by a silently aggressive policy, were becoming a power. The reign of Victor Amadeus I., who married the daughter of Henry IV, is remembered by the extinction of that religious sect called the Waldenses, a form of Protestantism, so named for its founder, one Peter Waldo. To escape persecution these people had hidden under the shadow of the Alps in Savoy and Piedmont, where, unobserved, they built their villages, and worshipped unmolested. After the Revocation of the Edict of Nantes, Victor Amadeus was ordered by Louis XIV to compel his Waldensian subjects to become Catholics, and between the armies of France and of Savoy, this picturesque and defenceless people were awakened from their dream and annihilated. It was soon after this that Louis also, upon a shallow pretext, bombarded and captured Genoa, converted its palaces into ruins, and then compelled the Doge and four chief senators to come in robes of state, kneel at his feet, and beg for pardon. When centralized authority had reached this point, it seems as if the time should have been ripe for something better than absolutism! And that something was already on its way, and making good progress, while Louis XIV and Louis XV were inviting the inevitable crisis which must attend overstrained authority. In the game of shuttlecock being played in Italy, when cities and states were tossed without ceasing from one to another, Nice was at this time also torn by Louis from Savoy, thus changing masters for the eighth time since 1387!

A vacant throne in Spain was for Italy of more importance than events nearer home. With the peace of Utrecht and the accession of Louis's grandson, Philip V., the astute Amadeus, Duke of Savoy, still further strengthened his house by the marriage of his two daughters, one with the new King of Spain and the other with the Duke of Burgundy, son and heir of Louis XIV. The settlement of this question of the Spanish succession at Utrecht, 1713, again upset the established boundaries in Italy. Spain had to give up Naples, which, with Milan and the island of Sardinia, was assigned to the disappointed Emperor of Germany. The Duke of Savoy, always on the winning side, in spite of the domestic ties uniting their families, had joined the grand alliance against Louis XIV. in the day of his decline. He had earned a reward, and so in the final distribution a long-coveted strip of territory between Milan and Genoa fell to him, and also the island of Sicily, with the title of King of Sicily. This he was induced in 1720 to exchange with the German Emperor for Sardinia, the regal title being changed to "King of Sardinia." It was in 1735, after the war of the Polish Succession, that Naples was returned to Spain and for twenty-one years ruled by Charles III, son of Philip V, and it was during this reign that the cities of Herculaneum and Pompeii were uncovered (1738 A.D.) after having been hidden for seventeen hundred years.

One seemingly unimportant exchange of territory at the time profoundly affected the future of Europe. The island of Corsica belonged to Genoa, and had for generations been struggling to free itself from the tyranny it hated. The impoverished and expiring republic in 1768, being in desperate need of money, sold her troublesome dependency to France; and so the Great Corsican, Napoleon Bonaparte, instead of being born an Italian, as he would have been, or a German, or a Spaniard, as he might have been, was a Frenchman!

The French people were the most plastic and receptive of any European nation, and required a steady hand to govern them. It is the effervescent wines and the volatile drugs that have to be tightly corked! But while kings and ministers could repress the manifestation of discontent, they could not prevent its existence, nor the increasing volume of vicious energies it generated. The problem set for each succeeding reign was to find the amount of external force required to imprison the forces within; each reign needing an increase of rigidity on the surface, and this in turn generating a greater volume of resistance from below, where destructive energies were looking for opportunity to escape. Such was the process from the death of Henry IV to Louis XVI. Richelieu, Mazarin, and Louis XIV, great and wise though they were, seem to have been ignorant of one philosophic truth— that nothing that is rigid endures.

A handful of people across the Atlantic, because of infringements upon their rights and liberties which would have seemed small indeed in France, had been measuring their strength with England—had cast off her yoke and joined the nations of the earth as a free and independent people. This was an object-lesson which made despots tremble and which wrought changes terrible but beneficent. The catastrophe long impending in France came in 1789, shaking Europe to its centre. The reign of absolutism was passing, and the day ushered in by a Renaissance was approaching its high noon.

It is characteristic of genius to see opportunity where to others is only a blank. Napoleon Bonaparte, with instinctive consciousness, saw the path to power. The air was vibrating with the word liberty. If he would capture the sympathies of France and of the world, he must move along the line of political freedom. The note to be struck is freedom for oppressed peoples. Where would he find chains more galling, servitude more unnatural, than in Italy? It mattered not whether kings liked it or not, there was a power abroad stronger than kings!

Without money, with an unpaid, unclothed army, he obeyed the inspiration. In 1796, with the unexpectedness of a tornado, he swept down upon the plains of Lombardy. The battles of Lodi, Areola, Rivoli, were won, and in ten months Napoleon was master of Italy, something no one man had been before since the fall of the Empire. By the treaty of Campo Formio, Northern Italy was divided into four republics—the Cisalpine, Ligurian, Cispadane, and Tiberine, with their capitals respectively at Milan, Genoa, Bologna, and Rome. Venetia, that is, Venice and its surrounding territory, was thrown into the lap of Austria, while what had been the Neapolitan Kingdom, or Southern Italy, had become the Parthenopean Republic, with its capital at Naples. When we see what this young, inexperienced general accomplished aa if by magic, how by a few phrases about "Liberty," and the "breaking of chains," addressed to Italians, and a few startling victories addressed to the Austrians, he had in ten months made himself master of all Italy, we are filled with wonder—not so much that he did it, as that neither Spaniard, German, nor Frenchman, singly or In alliance, bad been able to do it, although trying for three centuries.

What an opportunity was here for this man, in whose veins there coursed only Italian blood, to accomplish the dream of centuries—the unification of Italy! But his ambitions were too colossal for such an object, Italy was only the stepping-stone to a larger mastery. The people whose "chains" he had "come to break," were at once required to surrender territory, money, jewels, plate, horses, equipments, besides the choicest of their art collections and rare MSS. In a private letter to a member of the Directory, Napoleon writes: "I shall send you twenty pictures by the first masters—by Correggio and Michel Angelo." And later he says: Join all these to what will be sent from Rome, and we shall have all that is beautiful in Italy, except a small number of objects at Turin and Naples." Pius VI, without a protest, had surrendered his millions of francs and his MSS. and his ancient bronzes, and a part of Romagna—the papal territory. But he absolutely refused to recognize the existence of a "Tiberine Republic." Such recognition meant a renunciation of his temporal sovereignty. So the old man, trembling under the burden of years, was escorted over the border into France, where, after less than a year of captivity, he died (1799 AD). In 1804, after having himself proclaimed Emperor of the French, Napoleon came to Milan and placed upon his own head the Iron Crown of Lombardy. If Charlemagne was a successor of the Caesars, he was now the successor of Charlemagne, and Italy was his kingdom. He might do with his own as he liked. So, instead of consolidating, he broke it up once more into fragments. Eugene Beauharnais, his stepson, as viceroy of the Ligurian and Cisalpine republics (Lombardy and Piedmont), wore the title, King of Italy. The throne of Naples he gave to his brother, Joseph Bonaparte, to be transferred to his brother-in-law, Marshal Joachim, when to Joseph at a later time was assigned the throne of Spain, The Grand Duchy of Tuscany became a kingdom of Etruria with a Bourbon prince upon its throne. Ancient boundaries and landmarks were obliterated, geographical lines of separation removed, political divisions redistributed and rechristened, so that mediaeval Italy had disappeared. In other words, Napoleon accomplished in Italy just what he did later in Germany. In breaking down the revered old enclosures and tyrannies, he performed in a decade the work of centuries, and swiftly prepared the soil for a new order of things.

Pius VII, like his predecessor, refused to recognize the authority of the empire in his papal territory, so he, too, was carried into France, and Romagna was declared a part of the French Empire. But the period of a Napoleonic despotism was beneficent. Uniform laws were administered and equal rights conceded. Public works gave employment to the poor and public offices were open to all Italians, while to Jews and Protestants was given protection. An honest effort was made to reform the wretched peninsula, although at the same time draining it of its wealth and its youth by taxes, and conscription for Napoleon's colossal wars.

Chapter X

By the year 1815 Waterloo had been fought, Napoleon was at St. Helena, and the Allies were tearing down the temporary thrones and decorations. The proclamation of the Austrian general to the people of Italy in 1814, sounds as if it might have been copied from Napoleon's in 1796 "Italians! You have groaned long enough under the yoke of oppression. We have come to free you. Behold in us your liberators! Soon your lot will be envied. It is time the Alps should proudly raise an insurmountable barrier against oppression!" In the following way were these promises fulfilled: The statesmen assembled at the Congress at Vienna as far as possible restored the worst of the old tyrannies, with the addition of a few new ones. The Neapolitan Bourbons were replaced on the throne of Naples, including Sicily as before. The papal sovereignty and territory were restored. The old Hapsburg House returned to the Grand Duchy of Tuscany—Parma and Modena reappeared as independent duchies. Savoy was returned to King Victor Emmanuel I. of Piedmont, who also received, in addition, the territory belonging to the ancient Republic of Genoa. Venice had already been bestowed upon Austria by Napoleon—to this was now added Milan, making the Lombardo-Venetian Kingdom. And the duchy of Parma was given to the Austrian Princess Marie Louise, and Modena was restored to the Austrian tyrant Francis IV., who had trampled upon it long before the Napoleonic era. So over a great region comprising the fairest and richest part of Italy was written the name of the Austrian Empire, and for the domination of a Napoleon there was substituted the dominion of Austria—the most autocratic despotism in Europe.

Two parties arose in Italy, the Liberals and the Carbonari. The overthrow of Austrian tyranny was the object of both, the one by moderate measures, the other anarchistic. The Carbonari, with only indefinite ideas of the form of government to be substituted, pledged themselves to obey their leaders, and if necessary by violence and treachery to accomplish their freedom. This contributed the unthinking element which served to keep alive the tires of revolt, while the Liberals more reasonably and intelligently divided upon the relative wisdom of constitutional monarchy, or a republic, and the question of the temporal rule of the Pope. In opposition to these two parties was created another, the "Sanfedesti," or upholders of the Holy Faith, which taught absolute devotion to the Pope and death to Liberalism.

These were the three standards under which the battle was fought, while Austrian tyranny was striving to extinguish every aspiration toward liberty in the peninsula, the sovereigns in the states not absolutely hers being in fact simply her agents. When the feeble King of Naples yielded to a demand for a constitutional government, for which his people had been "teas-"teasing him," an Austrian army promptly appeared, took possession of the city, eight hundred Neapolitans were condemned to death, and many times that number sent to prisons and the galleys, the executioners becoming exhausted in their tasks! In this way was the promise made by the Austrian general in 1814 fulfilled in 1820! In this way was the yoke of oppression" broken by their "Liberators." At this same time (1820) there was a popular uprising in Piedmont. The cities demanded two things: a constitution, and freedom from Austria. King Victor Emmanuel I was sternly forbidden by Austria to yield a single point. His people were in rebellion. Rather than take up arms against them, he abdicated. In the absence of his brother, Charles Felix, his cousin, Charles Albert, was appointed Regent. The sympathies of the Regent were with the people, and he granted the constitution they prayed for. Charles Felix returned, repudiated the act, ordered his cousin to leave Turin and to go to the Austrian camp at Novara, where the officers received him with the shout intended to be derisive, but which was in fact so prophetic—"Behold the King of Italy!" Victor Emmanuel II, the Liberator, and the first real king of Italy since Theodoric, then an infant one year old in his cradle, was the son of this Charles Albert! The story of Naples was repeated. Instead of freedom and a constitution, death and imprisonment and exile were liberally bestowed until "quiet" was restored in Piedmont.

In the Romagna there had been worse Popes than Leo XII, but his ferocity may be imagined, when it is said that in the year 1825 five hundred and eight persons were beheaded for real or suspected Liberalism. The month of August witnessed the heaviest part; no less than three hundred executions taking place in that month, the list of victims including nobles, men of various professions, priests, and farmers. He also forbade vaccination while small-pox was raging, and set up the Inquisition to purge his kingdom of Jews and Protestants.

The Ghetto, to which the Jews had long been restricted, was a district on the banks of the Tiber separated from the city by walls. From the frequent overflow of the river and from neglect, its condition was indescribably shocking. Within this enclosure all the Jews were locked every evening, never, even in times of inundation, being permitted to sleep outside. These unfortunate people were not allowed to forget that they were only the offscourings of creation! At the opening of the carnival every year a deputation composed of Jews were compelled to present themselves at the capital, kneel abjectly at the feet of the "senator," and ask if they might be permitted to live! To which, after spurning them with his foot, the Christian magistrate answered with the usual formula: "'Go; for this year we will tolerate you!" The walls of this inferno, in which the unfortunate beings were confined, had become decayed, and the enforcement of the rules lax. So Leo XII. repaired the Ghetto and restored the waning discipline and the old order—as he would have done in every place where the air of freedom was getting access, in the land he would have liked to carry back into medievalism. The Duke of Modena, Francis IV., was another incarnation of tyranny. When a constitutional uprising appeared in his duchy in the form of a mild request, he sent the following note to the Austrian governor nearest him: "A terrible conspiracy against me has broken out. The conspirators are in my hands. Send me the hangman, Francis." In Bologna an uprising against the temporal authority of the Pope was successful—but the omnipresent Austrian was there in time to stamp it out. The teachings of the Sanfedesti may be inferred by the following extract from a manual introduced into Italian schools, entitled, "Duties of Subjects toward their Sovereigns." It proceeds in the form of a catechism:

Q. How should subjects behave toward their sovereign?
A. Subjects should behave like faithful slaves toward their master.
Q. Why should subjects behave like slaves?
A. Because the sovereign is their master and has as much power over their possessions as over their lives.

By such means as this did Austria try to secure the loyalty of a people chafing under her yoke, a people who were for the first time being drawn into a fraternal union with each other by the bond of a common hatred and a common aim—an emancipation from Austria.

In 1830 the hopes of patriots everywhere were strengthened, when Charles X, the last Bourbon king in France, was driven out, and Louis Philippe, a constitutional king, ascended the throne. There were at this time in Piedmont four youths whom Italy and the world could ill have spared! The kingdom over which that lover of Austria, Charles Felix, reigned, was the birthplace of liberty. Mazzini, the so-called Prophet of the Revolution, was born at Genoa, 1805; Garibaldi, its Soldier, at Nice, 1808; Cavour, its Statesman, at Turin, 1810, and Victor Emmanuel, the future El Galantuomo, also at Turin, in 1820. Charles Felix, or Carlo Feroce (Charles the Ferocious), as he was derisively called, died leaving no heir. Charles Albert had the nearest hereditary claim, but his liberal tendencies made him objectionable. Prince Metternich, the Austrian Minister, tried to arrange a marriage which would bring the troublesome kingdom of Piedmont into subjection. If the daughter of the deceased king married Francis IV. of Modena, the Salic law might easily be abrogated, and Piedmont would have a safe conservative guardian in the Duke of Modena, the most arbitrary ruler in Italy. The plan was a very ingenious one, but Talleyrand, Minister to Louis Philippe, did not approve of it, and so it came about that Charles Albert, who since the affair of the Constitution, in 1820, had been quietly at home teaching his boys to ride, and speak the truth, ascended the throne of his ancestors. But, unhappily, Charles Albert had permitted his hands to be tied before he took the reins, by a promise to the dying king that he would not disturb the form of government. Unconscious of this, Mazzini, believing the time was now ripe, called together his "Young Italy," to meet the Austrian onslaught which would undoubtedly come; never dreaming that the king would hesitate to grant the Constitution he so readily bestowed in 1890, as regent. The disappointment was bitter. The army of "Young Italy" found itself fighting not the Austrians, but the liberal King on whom their hopes had rested. Executions and imprisonments, and a price set upon Mazzini's head, were the punishment for trying to force a constitution upon a king who was under a pledge not to grant it, a secret compact which was to make the early part of his reign incomprehensible to patriots, and miserable to himself. But the time was coming when this well-intentioned and liberty-loving sovereign would free himself from the Austrian web spun about his throne, and would boldly ally himself with the cause of "Italy for Italians."

Chapter XI

The fifteen years of the pontificate of Gregory XVI. was a dreary period for patriots —Mazzini in England, and Garibaldi in South America, each with a price upon his head, Austrian bayonets always within call to quell uprisings; it needed faith of no common sort to believe the future held anything for Italy but degrading servitude to the Hapsburgs. In 1846 the conservative Gregory, the ardent upholder of Hapsburg rule, died. Who should be selected as his successor was a burning question. The choice fell upon Cardinal Feretti so unexpectedly to him that it was said when the result became certain he exclaimed, "Gentlemen, what have you done?" and then fainted. A gracious, smiling pope with liberal tendencies was received by the people with frantic joy. The ambassador hastening from Vienna with the Emperor' s veto, arrived too late. Pius IX was in the chair of St. Peter, and had commenced the pontificate which was to be a struggle between generous inclinations and what he considered his paramount duty as the custodian of the honor and sanctity of the Church, a natural dislike of foreign domination feebly clashing with an unwillingness to take up arms against a state so inflexibly loyal to the Church as Austria, and a determination that, come what would to the spiritual, the temporal authority of his office must be held intact. It was this eager grasp upon the temporalities which tainted all of this Pope's mental processes, and which made the long pontificate of Pius IX., covering one of the most critical periods, a tissue of unfortunate mistakes.

The new pontiff came at a time when, more than ever before, the hands of Italian patriots needed to be strengthened. Poland had been effaced in her despairing struggle with Russia, and Polish exiles were scattering seeds of rebellion wherever there were souls thirsting for freedom. There was something in the air of Europe which made despots uneasy. Patriots had grown bold not alone in Poland but in Hungary, and Italy was catching the contagion. Mazzini and Garibaldi were watching from afar so that they might return and join in the rescue. At this moment the fall of the monarchy and establishing of a republic in France sent an electric thrill throughout Europe. It was the French mode of saying that their government should have aided the cause of freedom in Poland and in Italy, and a warning to despotisms not to go too far! News of an insurrection in Vienna and the expulsion of Prince Metternich aroused the Milanese to make an attempt for their escape. "The time has come!" were the words with which they called upon the people to make a bold strike for liberty. Then it was that Charles Albert freed himself from his entanglement. A constitution was given to his people, and with his two sons, the Dukes of Savoy and Genoa, he threw himself into the struggle with Austria for the freedom of the Lombardo-Venetian Kingdom, The patriotic contagion spread, Tuscany, and even Rome, and at last Naples, sending troops to defend their Lombard brothers and the frontier of Italy. This is the sort of thing that makes patriotism! Never had a united Italy seemed so near. It needed only a great military leader—Napoleon in a day could have made Italy free. But there was no Napoleon, and there came a defeat at Custozza, and then a retreat to Milan - one red-shirted band of patriots, led by Garibaldi and Mazzini, stubbornly refusing to lay down their arms.

Pope Pius IX had not yet given his sanction to the movement, although none doubted that he would. Great was the shock when he issued an encyclical, April 29, 1848, saying he could take no part in a contest against Austria. The cause had received a terrible blow. The excitement at Rome was intense, the Pope's Minister was assassinated, and Pius IX fled in disguise under cover of the darkness to Gaeta, a fortified city on the coast near Naples.

Charles Albert resolved to make one more effort for the expulsion of Austrian troops from Lombardy. He met a crushing defeat at Novara, March 23, 1849. The Austrians followed the retreating army into Piedmont, with victory still more overwhelming upon his own soil. Charles Albert, unable to endure his humiliation and disappointment, abdicated, before he left the battlefield, in favor of his son, Victor Emmanuel, leaving to younger and stronger shoulders the burden too difficult and too heavy for him. The youth of only twenty-nine upon whom had descended this burden, undaunted by his father's despair, with set face looking out on the gloomy battle-field, uttered the words he was going to make true after twenty-one years of unceasing effort— "And yet, Italy shall be!"

Austria was in high spirits, and her efficient General Haynau was despatched to settle matters with the people in Lombardy. The town of Brescia, which had also evinced a taste for liberty, received the first lesson. The details of the burnings, and whippings, and wholesale slaughter so horrified people in England, that on the occasion of his visit there at a later time, when he had still further distinguished himself in Hungary, a mob took him in charge and thrashed him until he was rescued by the police; Tuscany, which now had its constitution and had been aiding in the war against Lombardy, was suddenly abandoned by her Grand Duke Leopold, who fled from Florence and joined the Pope and the King of Naples at Gaeta. The astonished people implored him to return, which he did only at a later time, when

Florence was garrisoned by Austrian troops, and the constitution and all the concessions to the spirit of freedom had vanished. Mrs. Browning's Casa Graidi Windows tells the story of Florence at this period, when a wave of returning despotism was the natural result of the overwhelming defeat of Charles Albert in Lombardy. Patriotism again began to hide its head, and the day of independence was farther off than ever. That antiquated despotism at Vienna believed that by fastening down all the valves, and permitting no steam to escape, the danger was averted! An uprising in Naples was put down with horrible barbarities. Houses were set on fire and women and children leaping from the windows were butchered in the streets below, which were actually running with blood, the Bourbon King Ferdinand making not the slightest effort to stay the massacre. Austria with her new young King, Francis Joseph, had her hands full at this time, with a great rebellion in Hungary incited by Polish exiles. The Czar helped him to stamp out this fire which had been kindled by his own revolted subjects, and then the vanquished Hungarian patriots were turned over to Haynau to be taught loyalty to Austria.

At this dark hour in Italy, and when abandoned by the Pope, a temporary government was formed at Rome, for the conduct of the war with Austria, Mazzini and Garibaldi aiding in its organization. The abolition of the Inquisition was its first measure. As the emancipated victims were borne out into the blinding sunlight, a great cry arose, "Down with the Pope! Long live the Republic!" It was many centuries since that cry had been heard in Rome.

A Triumvirate was elected by the Assembly, composed of Mazzini, Armellini, and Saffi. After years of waiting in exile, Mazzini's hour had come. He was virtual dictator of a Roman Republic. Calm, patient with opposition, never petulant nor melodramatic, his was not the low order of passion which expends itself in noise and fury. Extravagant he certainly was, and intense. But it was the intellectual and fine intensity of an idealist and an enthusiast, who knew no way-station between tyranny and perfect liberty; no compromise with political expediency. In his hatred for Monarchy he would not have regretted the overthrow of a Constitutional Government in Piedmont, provided it could lead the people to rise in mass and to achieve complete Republican freedom. If he had hitherto been a dreamer of impossible dreams, Mazzini's speculative tendency was now held in check by an imperative demand for the practical. The young republic must vindicate itself, must by its wisdom and its fruits prove its right to exist, and leave no pretext for intervention from jealous European despotisms.

The Roman Republic with high hopes appealed to England and to France to sustain it. Louis Napoleon sent 8,000 men to Civita Vecchia not to "sustain the republic," but to effect a reconciliation with the Pope! It soon became apparent that French soldiers were there not as rescuers, but as jailers. While there was great satisfaction at Gaeta when news came that General Oudinot was attacking Rome, in France, so intense was the popular indignation, that Louis Napoleon was obliged to send M. de Lesseps to patch up a peace which would be acceptable to the Pope, to General Oudinot, to the republic, and to the French Assembly! This difficult negotiation failed, Oudinot being determined to reinstate the Pope without conditions. Which presents the nobler picture—Pius IX. surrounded by emissaries from all of Europe, the centre of Machiavellian diplomacy, and rejoicing in a foreign invasion which was mutilating the dome of St. Peter's, and the gallery of the Vatican—or Mazzini and Garibaldi and their small band of patriots, with desperate courage defending the city from a French army sent to coerce them back into servitude to Austria.

Garibaldi's 19,000 men, making up in enthusiasm what they lacked in experience, with splendid valor for one month defended the city against 35,000 trained veterans. On July 3, 1849, the brave leader was hastily summoned before the Assembly, and in answer to their question, was compelled to admit that the defence could no longer be continued. The Assembly ordered a surrender, then with stately gravity, and as if it were a dying bequest, they conferred Roman citizenship upon all who had aided in the defence of the republic, and after this their last act, solemnly and calmly, like the Roman Senators of old at the first Gaulic invasion, they remained at their posts until they should be driven out by French bayonets. Then, before the entry of the French army. Garibaldi assembled his soldiers, and dramatically invited whoever would to follow him to the end of the struggle. He said, "I have only hunger and danger to offer you, the earth for a bed, and the sun for a fire, let whosoever does not despair of the fortunes of Italy follow me." Of the three or four thousand patriots who accepted these stern conditions and passed out of the gates of Rome that night, only a handful survived to witness Italian independence. Proclaimed as outlaws, most of them were captured and shot before they reached Piedmont. Garibaldi's faithful and adored wife, Anita, whom he had romantically married in South America and who insisted upon sharing his hardships, died from exhaustion by the way. Even at Piedmont the haunted patriot could find no safe asylum, and his wanderings did not cease until he reached America.

It is a sad picture we have of Mazzini, pallid with suppressed excitement, and wandering aimlessly like one in a dream amid the wreck of his hopes, until hurried across the frontier by friends.

Venice, which in the general uprising had declared herself a republic, was the last to surrender. The terrible Haynau with 30,000 Austrians invested the city, in which 2,500 beleaguered patriots held out until famine and pestilence compelled a capitulation. The triumph of Austria was complete. Every place in the fair peninsula, except that little state in the northwest, had given up the struggle. Pius IX, victorious and content, returned to Rome (1850), Cardinal Antonelli, the implacable enemy of free institutions, was appointed his chief adviser, and the brief career of the Roman Republic was over.

Chapter XII

The reign of Victor Emmanuel II commenced in deep shadow. Not a ripple of enthusiasm greeted his coming. At Turin, his capital, he was received with frigid coldness. His father was dying of a broken heart in Portugal, and there was nothing to make him glad but his Queen and his two little boys, Humbert and Amadeus. His army was demoralized and chafing under defeat, his people bitterly disappointed and angry, an unfriendly parliament criticising his every act, with extreme radicals exasperated at his conservatism, and extreme reactionists denouncing the liberal tendencies which had brought ruin to the state. It needed a stout heart to take up the burden, and no little address to reconcile his people to the galling terms he had been obliged to accept—30,000 Austrians quartered in Piedmont, and a heavy money indemnity to be paid. It is not strange that the young man of thirty years became grave and abstracted, and there came into his face that expression of deep sadness which grew to be habitual in after years. He one day told his Minister d'Azeglio, that of all the professions, that of king was the last he would have chosen. D'Azeglio replied, "But there have been so few honest kings, what a grand thing it would be to head the list as Re Galantuomo?" (Honest king.) The words struck Victor Emmanuel's fancy, and soon after when the Census Register was brought him for his signature, under the head "Profession" he wrote—"*Re Galantuomo*," and thus gave himself the title by which he will always be remembered.

The assumption of the title of emperor by Louis Napoleon in 1852 extinguished all hope of aid from France to the cause of freedom in Italy, while it produced a corresponding elation at Vienna and St. Petersburg. It was intimated to Victor Emmanuel that two systems of government on the peninsula, one absolute and the other constitutional, was an inconvenience which Austria and Prussia could not much longer tolerate. D'Azeglio's spirited reply was, in effect, that the King was master in his own kingdom, and wished for no advice in what concerned the welfare of his people.

When this able Minister gave np his portfolio in 1852, one no less able took his place. Count Camillo di Cavour had from his young manhood been identified with the Liberal Party. He was not impetuous, not a fiery leader of armed patriots like Garibaldi, not an impassioned dreamer like Mazzini. He was a wary student of men and of conditions, who with a patriotism no less intense than theirs was going to deal with the sources of things. If the force of the steam is necessary to drive the engine, the hand of the skilled engineer is no less needed to open or to close the valves as changing conditions demand. Garibaldi's headlong patriotism blazed the way to freedom, but that freedom and Italian unity would never have been consummated without the inflexible steadiness of purpose and the calm, wise statesmanship of two men, Victor Emmanuel and Cavour, his Minister.

Perfectly in accord, these two determined at once upon a measure of reform in the Church which should include the suppression of monastic institutions, and the amenability of the clergy to civil instead of ecclesiastical courts, thus sharply defining the position of the King on the side of the anticlerical party. Pope Pius IX, undeterred by these assaults upon his temporal authority, and wishing to proclaim his unimpaired supremacy, ventured upon an unprecedented act. When in 1854, alone, without the advice of a Church council, he promulgated the dogma of the Immaculate Conception of the Virgin, he made the first addition to the doctrine of the Church since the Council of Trent (1563 a.d.).

All the conditions were thus becoming intensified. Not only between clericals and non-clericals was the chasm widening, but also the greater one between Austria and the King of Sardinia. A protest from Cavour on account of merciless severities carried on against suspected Liberals in Lombardy, who were pursued even into Piedmont, received no attention from Austria, and diplomatic intercourse was broken off. The advent of the Austrian Archduke Maximilian as Viceroy of the Lombardo-Venetian Kingdom is interesting only on account of his subsequent tragic career in Mexico. Appointed to take the post made vacant by the retirement of Field-Marshal Radetsky, the interesting and accomplished youth brought his young and lovely bride Carlotta, Princess of Belgium, to Milan. Two years were spent in the fruitless endeavor to do justice and show mercy, with a power behind him thwarting his large-minded and amiable purposes. Milan was only one of the way-stations in the pathetic life-journey of a prince unfitted by nature to represent a merciless despotism.

The Crimean War was in many ways a crisis in the affairs of Europe. France and England in 1854 joined the Sultan in a war to prevent Russian encroachments upon Turkish soil. Victor Emmanuel hoped more from constitutional England than from any other source. It was true that Lord Palmerston had studiously refrained from giving even a moral support to the Italian cause, but a recent incident awakened hope. When the Duke of Genoa, the brother of the King, visited England during the previous year, the gracious Queen Victoria presented him with a horse, saying: "I hope you will ride this in fighting the battles for the liberation of Italy!" Significant and encouraging words to take back to his royal brother at that time! One can only surmise that among the mixed motives impelling the King and Cavour to join in the struggle for Ottoman integrity was a natural desire to secure the friendship, and perhaps the gratitude, of England. But the astute Cavour also saw the advantage to little Piedmont from participating in a great international war. It was a bold but successful move. When the King of Sardinia's contingent of 15,000 men received the congratulations of Queen Victoria after the battle of Tchernaya, and when at the Congress of Paris, where the treaty was signed, Piedmont was accorded the same footing as the five great powers, Austria realized that times and conditions had changed in the peninsula, and that her despised neighbor had been admitted to the circle of the great family of nations.

The gallant young Duke of Genoa, who had expected to command the Sardinian troops in the Crimea, died of consumption while the war was in progress, leaving an infant daughter, Margherita, who was to be the future wife of Prince Humbert and the adored Queen of Italy. When in one month the King lost his mother, his wife, and his brother, and was thus overwhelmed with private griefs, the Church construed it into a swift punishment for his wicked anti-clerical policy. Even Cavour urged a more gradual extinction of the monastic houses, earning by his moderation the hatred of the radicals. But Victor Emmanuel was firm and the famous "Ratazzi bill" was passed.

A visit to Paris, where the King was honored with the most flattering reception from Louis Napoleon, and another to England, no less flattering, when Queen Victoria bestowed upon him the Order of the Garter, and the air resounded with his praises, doubtless strengthened the expectation of aid from those governments. But when all these beguiling courtesies were over, the French emperor could not be brought to a decision by the skilful Cavour, while Lord Palmerston frankly told him that England would not consider any proposition unfriendly to Austria The blow had fallen. If Italy was to be, she must work out her own problem of unity. The clerical party in the kingdom was growing and outnumbered the party of the King, "What will become of us," said Cavour, "if they undo the work of eight years?" The King replied: "Rather than yield, rather than beat a retreat now, I would go to America and become plain M. de Savoie." If France would not aid them for love of their cause, she must be bought. The relations with Austria were becoming every day more strained. While massing 200,000 men on the borders of Lombardy, she was insolently protesting against the king's increasing his forces beyond what was required for a peace-footing. There could be no peace and no starting-point for Italy's redemption until Victor Emmanuel was King of all Northern Italy.

Louis Napoleon needed two things to solidify his empire at home and abroad. He must have brilliant military successes to make Frenchmen forget the republic, and he must make distinguished royal alliances for his family to increase its prestige among other nations. A marriage between his cousin Jerome Bonaparte and the young Princess Clotilde, the daughter of Victor Emmanuel, just fifteen years old, was worth considering. So when privately sounded by Cavour as to the price he would ask for armed assistance to Sardinia, he named the two things most sacred and dear to the King, his ancestral duchy of Savoy and his daughter! In return for these, if the war was successful, the kingdom of Sardinia would include Lombardy and Venetia.

The King consented to the sacrifice, and in an address from the throne at Turin a few days later he uttered words which were correctly construed by an astonished Parliament as an announcement that he" was about to call the nation to army. The people were electrified. The applause in Parliament was frantic, men springing to their feet and shouting until they were hoarse, "Long live the King!" When he uttered the words, "we have heard the cry of anguish," words so eloquent of sympathy, and pity determined rescue, were caught up as a watchword throughout the peninsula, Victor Emmanuel, no longer distrusted, had conquered the hearts of his own people, and was the hope of every patriot in Italy.

The condition of the marriage was the one over which the King struggled longest, and not until his daughter's free consent was obtained did he accede to it, his Ministers assuring him the while that without it there would be no aid from France. So in the month of January, 1859, the nuptials were celebrated.

Chapter XIII

Italy was astir with expectancy and preparation. Francis Joseph peremptorily demanded that Victor Emmanuel should at once disband the Piedmontese army, allowing three days for a reply. This precipitated the crisis for which all were longing. Within a week the Austrian army had crossed the Ticino and a division of the French army was in Turin. Louis Napoleon, in his dramatic proclamation, said he came to "give Italy to herself," and that she was to be free "from the Alps to the Adriatic!"

With such a glorious promise what wonder that Garibaldi's volunteers drove the retreating Austrians through the defiles of the Lombard hills, and that the field at Magenta was won with an overwhelming victory. Never had Milan witnessed such a scene of wild rejoicing as when Louis Napoleon and Victor Emmanuel, with their victorious armies, entered the city adorned as for a bridal, with wreaths of flowers and gorgeous draperies of gold and silver brocade hanging from windows and balconies, the air ringing with shouts of a people rejoicing at their liberation. When the news of these victories was received, Leopold, Grand Duke of Tuscany, Francis, Duke of Modena, and the Duchess of Parma all fled to the protection of the Austrians, and the three rejoicing states immediately offered their allegiance to the "King of Italy." All the states in the papal territory which were governed by papal legates—that is, all except Rome and its immediate vicinity—in similar manner declared their desire for annexation. Nothing could have been swifter or more spontaneous than this obedience to the principle of unity in a new Italy, every freed atom at once trying to ally itself to the central authority.

In three weeks after Magenta came the crucial battle of Solferino. The fate of Italy hung upon that day—a day of long and desperate struggle. When the sun went down, Francis Joseph had been defeated. The quarters he had occupied in the morning were occupied at night by Louis Napoleon and his staff, the Emperor of Austria weeping it is said over the ruin of his hopes.

The rest of the way was easy. There was now only Venetia lying just before them, which there was no chance that the demoralized Austrians could hold, and the glorious promise would be fulfilled—Italy would be free "from the Alps to the Adriatic!"

But it was the unexpected that happened! Napoleon III, without consulting Victor Emmanuel, asked the vanquished Emperor Francis Joseph for an armistice.

"But, sire," said his marshal, "an armistice means peace."

"That is nothing to you," was the reply.

"But, sire," persisted the astonished marshal, "you promised to make Italy free from the Alps to the Adriatic."

"I repeat, sir, that is nothing to you."

No explanation was ever vouchsafed for this shameless betrayal of Italy by the man posing as her liberator; the man who had said the night before Magenta, "Be soldiers today, tomorrow you will be citizens of a great country!"

With brutal abruptness and with the brevity of a dictator, Louis Napoleon made known his terms to Victor Emmanuel. The King of Sardinia might have Lombardy, but Venetia remained with Austria, and Savoy and Nice must belong to France. The people were frantic. " We have been betrayed!" they shrieked.

"Betrayed and insulted," said Cavour. The Minister, normally so calm, so self-contained, paced the floor, his face white and drawn with the intensity of his anger. "Refuse Lombardy," he said to the King. "Better to cut loose from the traitor at once and let him take the consequences."

The King alone was firm and calm. Profoundly disappointed, profoundly miserable, he yet saw clearly that the path of wisdom was in the decision he was about to make. When the stormy interview of two hours was ended, the terms of the French Emperor were accepted and Cavour had resigned his portfolio.

And so the peace of Villafranca was signed, and the Emperor, Louis Napoleon, surprised at the coldness of his reception as he passed through the cities, returned to France impressed with the ingratitude of the Italians, to whom he had given Lombardy!

The study of human motives, always a complex and difficult one, is doubly so in a character so inscrutable as Louis Napoleon's, where the straight path was never taken and all things were done by indirection. Whether his amazing conduct was the result of political foresight and designed to prevent a European coalition against a too victorious France, or whether he concluded that two great victories were sufficient to give him the prestige he needed, none will ever be able to say. Statesmanship and philanthropy do not often go hand in hand in such transactions, but we do know that the parting effort of this "Liberator" was to force back Tuscany, Modena, Parma, and the Romagna into their old servitude to Austrian agents. On this point Victor Emmanuel was inflexible. He wrote to the Emperor: "We can succumb, but never betray. Rather than be unworthy of the love and confidence these noble and unfortunate people have reposed in me, I will break my sword and throw the crown away, as did my august father!"

It would not have surprised him at this juncture, if his late ally had joined with Austria to crush him. The situation needed steadiness and caution, and with admirable calmness and with perfect dignity he submitted to the cruel exigencies of a dangerous crisis. One can imagine how Garibaldi's heart was wrung, and how he impulsively resigned his commission in contempt for such a coldblooded king, and then as impulsively took it up again, vaguely intending to attack somebody, he knew not whom; somewhere, he knew not how; and then, impatient at being held in check, again threw down his sword, went to weep upon his adored Anita's grave, and retired to the little island of Caprera, which he had bought as a refuge with a legacy left him by his brother. The fate of the central states was the first matter to be adjusted. Victor Emmanuel, with his usual calmness of judgment, was slow to open the door at which they were knocking. There must be no loop-hole for suspicion which could be used against him by the wily agents of Austria, Prussia, France, and the Pope, who were whispering and conspiring at Naples to prevent the proposed annexation. But it was the embittered reproaches of Pius IX. which most disturbed the King. He wrote assuring the Holy Father of his undying devotion to him as a spiritual ruler, at the same time respectfully protesting against his policy in temporal matters, in defeating the desire of his subjects for a constitutional government. But with the King of Naples, his trusted confidant, and with Cardinal Antonelli, his counsellor, both whispering encouragement in his ear, Pius IX, stood firm and earned the admiration of haters of liberty everywhere. Aa time passed, the European states, wearied perhaps, or it may be moved by the logic of events, relaxed in their opposition. It was finally suggested by Cavour that they should settle the matter by recourse to a "plebiscite," a method in high favor with the Emperor of the French, The plan was accepted. A vote of the people in Tuscany, Modena, Parma, and the Papal States (those under legates) was overwhelmingly in favor of annexation, which was at once carried into effect. The temporal sovereignty of the Pope was now restricted to a small territory about Rome, and Victor Emmanuel was king of an Italy which extended not "from the Alps to the Adriatic," but from the Alps to the borders of the Papal and the Neapolitan kingdoms; an Italy which, as he said in his opening speech to his enlarged Parliament, was "not the Italy of the Romans, nor of the Middle Ages, but the Italy of the Italians." These borders did not satisfy the impatient patriot at Caprera, who was devising his own plans for their extension. Cavour, who had wisely resumed his portfolio, and had patiently labored with the Parliament to secure its consent to the treaty with the clause so odious to himself—the abandonment of Nice—was never forgiven by the uncompromising soldier, who bitterly said, "That man has made me a stranger in my own house." It was a kind fate which gave to Victor Emmanuel so wise a counsellor in those critical years, of whom Prince Metternich said: "There is but one statesman in Europe and he is against us. That one is M. de Cavour."

King Ferdinand of Naples, known as King Bomba, was dead and had been succeeded by his son, Francis II, because of his close imitation of his father's methods called "Bombina." So scandalous was the corruption in his government, so flagrant and so shameless the methods of the despotism at Naples, that France, Spain, and even autocratic Russia, urged him to pause and make peace with his outraged people before it was too late. We need not stop to tell the sickening details of imprisonment of suspects in dungeons, without light, without air, in an Italian midsummer, fighting in the darkness with rats— and this for a whispered criticism of the government, or a suspected inclination to liberalism, or a desire to unite their fortunes with the new kingdom in the North. It is not strange that Garibaldi, chafing in his solitude at Caprera, was roused to a desperate resolve.

This extraordinary man who had led the picturesque legion in the defence of the Roman Republic and had shown himself master of guerilla warfare in Lombardy, had also given no little anxiety to the King and Cavour. An eye had been constantly kept upon him since Novara, and a check-rein held always in hand to arrest headlong dashes toward centres of tyranny, to which he was addicted at most critical times. But if his methods were displeasing to them, theirs were exasperating to him. Diplomacy he despised. He would have cut every knot with the sword. Equally frank in his loves and his hatreds, he was as transparent as a child. Generous, simple, ardent, he possessed in a superlative degree those qualities which arouse a passionate devotion, and which convert followers into worshippers. Tossed from Italy to America, from America back to Italy, and thence to South America, whatever the vicissitudes of his life, it was always invested with a romantic charm. If he entered Montevideo as a drover of cattle, he left it the hero of daring exploits, of a romantic wooing, and the leader of armies against Spanish tyranny. If he was the maker of soap and of candles in Staten Island, he returned to his own land to accomplish the liberation of one-half of Italy by an act unmatched since the days of Roland.

No soldier of fortune in the Renaissance, not Sforza, nor Carmagnola, cast a greater spell over his followers than did this red-shirted leader over his adoring veterans, as, in the same strange South American garb, they sat at night about their bivouac-fires, or lassoed their untethered horses, apparently as undisciplined as wild colts, and yet alertly watching for a glance or a nod, and ready on the instant to do or to dare anything at his bidding.

How Piedmont sympathized with the Neapolitans it need not be said. But a single move toward their emancipation might bring France and Austria in combination against the growing power of the King of Sardinia. Gari-Garibaldi had no fear of consequences and no policies to embarrass him! His first purpose of recovering Nice was abandoned for that of freeing the kingdom of Naples. The Sardinian government wisely refrained from knowing much about the audacious enterprise, and in 1860, with his thousand volunteers, he embarked from Genoa. In two weeks he was inside the walls of Palermo, the people, frantic with joy, beating the bells with hammers all the day long, the royalists having removed the clappers to prevent such a demonstration of rejoicing. Garibaldi, now assuming the title of Dictator, pressed on, his little force growing with recruits and royalist troops melting away before him until he reached Messina, and the island was his.

Francis II was panic-stricken. He announced instantly his intention of giving a constitution to his people, and also wished to form an alliance with Piedmont. It was a death-bed repentance which came too late. He told the Dictator he might have Sicily, and he would also give him 50,000,000 francs to aid in the liberation of Venice, if he would leave the mainland alone. Victor Emmanuel, who had received an urgent letter from Louis Napoleon asking him to recall his imprudent general, wrote the Dictator that he thought they "should be content with Sicily," and instructed him to desist from an attack upon Naples. Garibaldi replied that, for just this once, he should disobey his orders, adding, "but when I shall have made you King of Italy, I will lay my sword at your feet, and obey you for the rest of my life." So, almost without money, except Mazzini's last 30,000 francs which he sent Garibaldi to convey his troops to Naples, and with a handful of men, and by sheer audacity and force of purpose, the kingdom of Naples was swept to the feet of the King of Sardinia. Austria, bankrupt and harassed by the Hungarians, offered no opposition, so there was no pretext for interference from Louis Napoleon. Francis II for a time held out at Gaeta, that old refuge for tyrants in extremity, then with a proclamation full of pathos, and with a dignity worthy of a better cause, he disappeared from view, dying in obscurity at Paris in 1895.

The 80,000 Neapolitan troops had disappeared like the snow before the sun. When Garibaldi entered Naples the people acted as if they had gone mad. For eight hours he had to appear and reappear on the balcony in response to their wild shouts and clamor, until from sheer exhaustion he had to retire for rest. Then like little children they whispered, "Our father sleeps, " and hushed and silent went about the streets holding their hands high above their heads with one finger pointing upward, a pantomime which had the glad meaning—"Italy is one!"

Chapter XIV

While this was taking place, Victor Emmanuel was attacking an enemy nearer home. Probably knowing the time was favorable for the undertaking, he sent an envoy to the Pope, respectfully but positively demanding the retirement of the foreign troops which he had called to his aid under General Lamoriciere. Pius IX refused to consider the request. Without hesitation, the King sent troops down into the papal territory and after a short campaign Lamoriciere and his foreigners were driven out. Catholic Europe was much scandalized by such a proceeding. Austria and Prussia and Russia joined in a chorus of angry protest, Louis Napoleon withdrew his Minister from Turin, and even from Gaeta there came a feeble little voice—that of Francis II, late King of Naples.

It was toward Gaeta that the King's army turned when matters were settled with Lamoriciere and his men. Near Naples Victor Emmanuel and Garibaldi met for the first time since the wonderful achievement. As they clasped each other's hands, Garibaldi, his voice choked with emotion, said, "King of Italy!" To which the King simply answered, "Grazie!" Then later gratefully telling the gallant soldier that his daring had hastened Italian unity by ten years. To which Garibaldi replied, "But, Sire, it could not have been done had not Victor Emmanuel been the most noble and generous of kings!"

Hoping for a republic no less eagerly than Mazzini, Garibaldi always yielded his own ardent and impatient desires to the necessities of the situation, while Mazzini, never diverted from his lofty ideal, hating a monarchy almost as much as he did Austrian tyranny, had for years embarrassed the government at every step. Again and again had he kindled revolutionary fires, leaving behind him a trail of conspiracies and revolts, followed by executions and exile, seriously damaging the cause for which he would have been glad to die. So this hour of exultation was one of bitterness and defeat to the brooding and disappointed idealist. When the more plastic Garibaldi, finding a republic was impossible, bestowed his splendid prize upon King Victor Emmanuel, the great opportunity was lost!

A plebiscite was taken and the desire of the people was unanimously expressed for annexation. So the soldier laid down his Dictatorship, left to Victor Emmanuel the kingdom he had captured, then returned to Caprera, as someone happily says, "to dig up in the fall the potatoes he had planted in the spring." It is an amusing picture we get of the hero's home—of his red shirts and gray trousers hung over a rope stretched across his bedroom, and a framed lock of Anita's hair hanging over his bed, and— most delicious touch of all—his three donkeys in the courtyard, named respectively Francis Joseph, Louis Napoleon, and Fio Nono!

In 1861 Victor Emmanuel opened his new Parliament, representing all of Italy except Venetia and Rome. It was only twelve years since Novara— since unloved and unwelcomed he came to Turin, and now, the centre of the hopes of the nation, he was "By the grace of God, and by the will of the people (the addition is his own), King of Italy."

His was not yet a bed of roses. The task imposed by the enormous addition of illiteracy and of helplessness and crime was not a simple one. The new census revealed the appalling fact that out of the 22,000,000 subjects now ruled by Victor Emmanuel, 17,000,000 could neither read nor write, while brigandage, incited and encouraged by royalists and by the agents of Francis II., prevailed to a frightful extent in the newly acquired territory. Cavour grasped all these difficulties and problems with the hand of a master, not the least of his tasks being to keep in check the irrepressible Garibaldi, always in conflict with sober methods, never forgetting that Cavour had given Nice, his native city, to France, and losing no opportunity to reproach him with words not easy to bear. But with sublime patience Cavour bore it all and strove to bring order out of a chaos of financial, military, and economic affairs, these complicated by the ever-persistent irritation arising from a Pope at Rome supported by a French garrison. The strain was prodigious, and within a year Cavour showed signs of breaking under it. It was with overwhelming grief that Victor Emmanuel stood at the bedside of his dying Minister in 1861.

"Better for Italy if it were I who had died!" were his words when all was over.

The impatient leader at Caprera was in the meantime planning a settlement of the vexed Roman question. When the King heard that he was in Sicily raising an army with the watchword "Rome or Death!" he immediately sent an armed force to stop the reckless proceeding. Garibaldi, wounded by Italian soldiers and under the displeasure of his King, in the very territory he had bestowed upon him, presents a spectacle confusing to the sensibilities and to the conscience of beholders! But it was an additional proof of Victor Emmanuel's calmness of judgment that he could deal promptly and wisely with a situation so painful. And a general amnesty proclaimed upon the marriage of his daughter, Maria Pia, with the young King of Portugal, relieved him of the necessity of punishing the soldier to whom he owed so much.

This reckless attempt increased the complication at Rome, Louis Napoleon strengthened his garrison, and Pius IX. took a fresh hold upon his temporal sovereignty. And when there came a petition signed by priests, praying the Holy Father to yield to the entreaties of his children and make peace with Victor Emmanuel, Cardinal Antonelli scornfully replied that his Holiness made no terms with robbers, and so could not treat with the "Robber King" at Turin. The new ministry went on with the work of reform. Schools were established, and a railway, that messenger of civilization, extended all the way down to Brindisi, the ancient city of Brundisium, just as the Appian Way that messenger of an ancient civilization had done long centuries before.

If Garibaldi had left his beloved Italy once more under a cloud, the cloud lifted when he arrived in London, and was given an ovation such as few heroes have received. He found himself the idol of the hour, and children and young maidens, in England and in America, were wearing the scarlet flannel blouse which bore his name. Perhaps it was this voice of approval which encouraged the reckless hero again and again to make the attempt, from which he only desisted when he saw his infatuated boys mowed down by French chassepots at the gates of Rome, having accomplished nothing except to greatly increase Victor Emmanuel's burden by rendering negotiations with Louis Napoleon impossible.

By the year 1866 the situation in Europe had been changed by the advent of a new and potent factor. Count Bismarck believed the time was ripe for Prussia to throw off the Austrian yoke, that antiquated assumption of headship which was the last surviving relic of a Holy Roman Empire! The old despotism at Vienna was much shaken since its conflicts with Hungary and Italy, and was not carrying things with so high a hand as it used to do. Bismarck rightly judged that a war at this time would result happily for Prussia. It mattered little what it was about. Fortune favored him by a dispute over the Danish duchies of Schleswig and Holstein, Austria claiming Holstein as her share of the spoils, after the defeat of Denmark by Austria and Prussia in 1864. So war was declared, Bismarck in advance having made a secret alliance, offensive and defensive, with Italy. Prince Humbert and his brother Amadeus, Duke of Aosta, did valiant service, but the Italians were badly beaten at Custozza. This was of little consequence, however. The event so long desired was coming through an unexpected door. The Austrians were totally defeated at Sadowa. Louis Napoleon was asked by Francis Joseph to act as mediator, receiving from him at the same time Venetia, to dispose of as he would. Here was an opportunity for the amende honorable. Seventy years before the great Napoleon had given the hapless Venice to Austria. Louis Napoleon himself had bitterly disappointed the

Italians in failing to recover it in 1859. Now, seven years later, he offered it aa a free gift to the country so wronged. So, with the consent of Count Bismarck, which Victor Emmanuel made a condition of its acceptance, Venetia was at last joined to Italy. Now there remained only the Eternal City. Europe was getting very tired of the subject of the "Papal Captivity." The relations between Austria and the Vatican had become less intimate, and as Francis Joseph withdrew his active sympathies from Pius IX. he made friendly overtures toward Italy. Pius IX., while promulgating his new dogma of Papal Infallibility (1870), and thus increasing the defences about his position, still made it plain that it was only the man who claimed to be King of Italy to whom he refused his friendship; that for Victor Emmanuel, the King of Sardinia, he felt the deepest regard. At the same time Victor Emmanuel lost no opportunity to assure the Holy Father of his undying devotion to him as the spiritual head of his kingdom and of Christendom. In the midst of these interchanges and the general softening of embittered hearts, the end was approaching, as it so often does, from an entirely unexpected source.

Napoleon III declared war against Prussia. The balance had been disturbed by the humiliation of his old ally, Austria, and he was going to restore it by vanquishing the victor—this Protestant Prussia, which stood for all that he was not. In seven weeks came Sedan (1870). The French Emperor was a prisoner and the French Empire had ceased to exist. There was no longer a French garrison at Rome.

In the correspondence which followed between Victor Emmanuel and the Pope, one respectfully expressed his determination to take possession of his capital, and the other an equal resolve to yield it only to superior force. Pius IX gave orders to his few French *zouaves* to capitulate as soon as a breach was made in the walls. That hour quickly arrived, and a white handkerchief fluttering from the point of a bayonet announced that the end had come—that Rome was joined to Italy, and the unification which had been the dream of centuries was accomplished.

In the altered European conditions not one state remained to protest against this climax. The French Empire had vanished, Prussia was now the ally of Italy, and when the Pope appealed to his old friend and champion, Austria, to protect him from this invasion of his rights and territory, the reply promptly came that Austria could do nothing to interrupt the friendly relations with Italy which she was happy to say had existed since their reconciliation. So Pius IX proclaimed himself a prisoner, and during the seven years of life remaining to him never stepped beyond the precincts of the Vatican. By what is known as "The Law of the Papal Guarantees," the sovereign pontiff is accorded royal honors and a revenue of $645,000. His person is as inviolable as the King's. The Vatican and Lateran palaces, with their grounds and all the works of art contained in them, are for his exclusive use as is also the Castel Gandolfo, his summer palace. These places are sacredly his own. No official under any circumstances can enter them without his permission. The jurisdiction thus afforded by the Papal Guarantees is over the church property in the city of Rome, and six suburban sees which were reserved by the government for the papal use. To these limits is the "temporal sovereignty" of the Pope restricted.

In 1869 a son was born to Prince Humbert and Margherita, the charming cousin he had married the year before. The boy was christened Vittorio Emmanuel and received the title of Prince of Naples. The King's other son, Amadeus, Duke of Aosta, had been invited to fill a vacant throne in Spain and had commenced his dreary experiment of playing the part of Re Galantuomo in that country. In July, 1871, the royal residence was removed from the temporary capital at Florence, and amid great rejoicings was established at the Quirinal palace in Rome. An incident is described in connection with this event which brings into strong and pathetic relief characters who have since passed off the stage of human events. Emperor Frederick of Germany, at that time the adored Unser Fritz, had been invited to make one of the party at the Quirinal on that occasion. When the royal family appeared upon the balcony he impulsively snatched up the little prince, who is now the King of Italy, and to the terror of his mother, held him up high in his arms in view of the tumultuous, shouting throng below.

Chapter XV

One by one the principal actors in the drama of Italy's unification dropped by the way. In 1872 Mazzini, the irreconcilable patriot and the "prophet of the Revolution," died at Pisa. In 1879 an unexpected and stunning blow fell upon the people. Victor Emmanuel was stricken with a fatal illness. Pope Pius IX., deeply moved, sent word that he was only prevented by age and infirmities from coming himself to administer the last rites, which he sent a cardinal to perform. Princess Clotilde and Amadeus were quickly summoned, but arrived too late. The *Re Galantuomo* was no more. A cry of poignant grief ascended from the whole of Italy. People wept as for a father. King Humbert's proclamation, issued a few hours after the death of the King, closed with these words: "Italians—Your first King is dead. His successor pledges himself to prove to you that constitutions do not die!"

Modern Rome had witnessed nothing like the scene at the funeral as their dead King passed from the Quirinal to the Pantheon—the "Iron Crown of Lombardy" borne on a cushion behind the coffin.

Just one month later Pius XX., the "prisoner of the Vatican," was dead, and, lying in his splendid vestments, was borne to St. Peter's, and placed in the niche which for thirty-two years had been occupied by Gregory XVI. Cardinal Pecci, who was chosen by the conclave, took the name Leo XII, and commenced the pontificate which still continues. The course pursued by Pius IX has not been materially altered. Leo XIII is still the "prisoner of the Vatican," and performs no religious ceremonies except in the Sistine Chapel and in St. Peter's.

The splendid intelligence of this Pope, and the modernness of his intellectual spirit, have many times led the world to believe he was on the verge of tearing down some of the old walls of separation, and letting the currents of a modern world course through the veins of the Church. But just as many times has the world been disappointed. Few men, be they popes, emperors, or kings, are strong enough to defy the traditions of the exalted place to which they have been called. Whether there has been such a conflict as is implied by this in the mind of the venerable and extraordinary man who occupies the chair of St. Peter today, no one knows. But to some it has seemed so. And it has also seemed that he has lost an opportunity of making his pontificate memorable by infusing a new life into the Church. The reconciliation with the King of Italy and that other reconciliation with the scientific spirit of the age which would so have advanced the interests of the Church and made this pontificate so memorable, have not come.

The reign of King Humbert is too near to be treated historically, but the love he had won from Italy was attested when on July 29, 1900, he was cruelly assassinated by the anarchist Brescia. A cry of horror and of grief arose from his entire kingdom. It was not an easy thing to succeed Victor Emmanuel, and Humbert had borne himself well for twenty-two years under trying difficulties. With no great sources of wealth such as are possessed by other lands, with an undeveloped peasant population disproportionately large, with a burdensome taxation necessary to meet the expenses of the government, and with earthquakes, and floods, and cholera, the King of Italy had no sinecure.

The national finances demanded wisdom in the rulers, and patient sacrifice from the people. The maintenance of a sovereign pontiff in royal state at Rome is a heavy burden for a state so encumbered to bear. And as their guest is an unwilling one, the usual compensations for expensive entertainment do not exist! The many irritations growing out of this hostility between the Quirinal and the Vatican necessarily make the throne of Italy a very uneasy seat. For two luminaries to try to shine in close proximity to each other in a small corner of the heavens, would be a similar experiment. Rome is not large enough for two thrones, especially if one of these claims the earth.

A small cloud in 1891 obscured the peaceful relations which have always subsisted between Italy and the United States. Eleven Italians belonging to the secret society of the "Mafia" were murdered by an exasperated mob in New Orleans. It was discovered that only two of these men were Italian citizens, and the matter was finally adjusted by Marquis di Rudini and Secretary Blaine, through the skilful mediation of Baron Fava, the sum of S25,000 being paid by the United States to the families of the two murdered men. The name Mafia is said to have come from the initials of the war-cry at the time of the Sicilian Vespers—"Morta Alia Francesi Italia Ancla." M. A. F. I. A. A mixture apparently of Italian with Sicilian dialect. The word Mafia has degenerated until it signifies any association for purposes of vengeance.

Upon the tragic death of Humbert, the infant held aloft in the strong arms of "Unser Fritz" twenty-nine years before was King of Italy. While we are writing these words the bells in Rome are ringing and there is rejoicing at the Quirinal Palace over the birth of a daughter to the King and Queen Helena, his beautiful Montenegrin bride.

Italy has had more than its share of rich human experiences, any one of which would have bestowed immortality. The list is an imposing one. A Roman Republic, a Roman Empire, the triumphs of her medieval cities, when her merchant princes ruled the commerce of the world, the emancipation of human thought by the Renaissance, the production of the world's masterpieces in art, and last of all, the most dramatic of modern epics, the struggle which resulted in the unification of Italy! Do the annals of the Italian peninsula record anything nobler than this achievement!

THE END

Printed in Great Britain
by Amazon